NEW ESSAYS ON *BILLY BUDD*

The American Novel series provides students of American litera-ture with introductory critical guides to great works of American literature. Each volume begins with a substantial introduction by a distinguished authority on the text, giving details of the work's composition, publication history, and contemporary reception, as well as a survey of the major critical trends and readings from first publication to the present. This overview is followed by a group of new essays, each specifically commissioned from a leading scholar in the field, which together constitute a forum of interpretative methods and prominent contemporary ideas on the text. There are also helpful guides to further reading. Specifically designed for undergraduates, the series will be a powerful resource for anyone engaged in the critical analysis of major American novels and other important texts.

Billy Budd is Herman Melville's most read work after *Moby-Dick*, and it is regularly taught in literature courses of all kinds. Melville wrote the novella during the five years before his death, and it was published posthumously in 1924. The essays collected here investigate *Billy Budd* in the context of nineteenth-century political and social dynamics and the literary response they pro-voked, as well as the relevance of mythology and the histories of the classical world and Judaeo-Christian civilization to Melville's book. Also examined are Melville's later writing, including the late poetry; the text's development; and its ambiguities. The collec-tion will prove an invaluable resource for students of this major American writer.

Donald Yannella, a noted scholar of American Romanticism, is the author of *Ralph Waldo Emerson* and co-author of *Herman Melville's Malcolm Letter*, among other books; he edited *Extracts*, the Melville Society quarterly, for fifteen years.

✳ The American Novel ✳

GENERAL EDITOR
Emory Elliott
University of California, Riverside

Other works in the series:

NEW ESSAYS ON *BILLY BUDD*

EDITED BY

DONALD YANNELLA

3 1257 01556 1219

PUBLISHED BY THE PRESS SYNDICATE OF THE UNIVERSITY OF CAMBRIDGE
The Pitt Building, Trumpington Street, Cambridge, United Kingdom

CAMBRIDGE UNIVERSITY PRESS
The Edinburgh Building, Cambridge CB2 2RU, UK
40 West 20th Street, New York, NY 10011-4211, USA
477 Williamstown Road, Port Melbourne, VIC 3207, Australia
Ruiz de Alarcón 13, 28014 Madrid, Spain
Dock House, The Waterfront, Cape Town 8001, South Africa

http://www.cambridge.org

First published 2002

Printed in the United Kingdom at the University Press, Cambridge

Typeface Fournier 12.5/14 pt.   *System* LaTeX 2ε [TB]

A catalogue record for this book is available from the British Library

ISBN 0 521 41778 3 hardback
ISBN 0 521 42829 7 paperback

To the new innocents,
our grandchildren,
Julia, Kate, Peter,
Elizabeth, Margaret,
Lena, Helen, et al. fut.

Contents

Series Editor's Preface

In literary criticism the last twenty-five years have been particularly fruitful. Since the rise of the New Criticism in the 1950s, which focused attention of critics and readers upon the text itself – apart from history, biography, and society – there has emerged a wide variety of critical methods which have brought to literary works a rich diversity of perspectives: social, historical, political, psychological, economic, ideological, and philosophical. While attention to the text itself, as taught by the New Critics, remains at the core of contemporary interpretation, the widely shared assumption that works of art generate many different kinds of interpretations has opened up possibilities for new readings and new meanings.

Before this critical revolution, many works of American literature had come to be taken for granted by earlier generations of readers as having an established set of recognized interpretations. There was a sense among many students that the canon was established and that the larger thematic and interpretative issues had been decided. The task of the new reader was to examine the ways in which elements such as structure, style, and imagery contributed to each novel's acknowledged purpose. But recent criticism has brought these old assumptions into question and has thereby generated a wide variety of original, and often quite surprising, interpretations of the classics, as well as of rediscovered works such as Kate Chopin's *The Awakening*, which has only recently entered the canon of works that scholars and critics study and that teachers assign their students.

The aim of the American Novel Series is to provide students of American literature and culture with introductory critical guides to American novels and other important texts now widely read and studied. Usually devoted to a single work, each volume begins with an introduction by the volume editor, a distinguished authority on the text. The introduction presents details of the work's composition, publication history, and contemporary reception, as well as a survey of the major critical trends and readings from first publication to the present. This overview is followed by four or five original essays, specifically commissioned from senior scholars of established reputation and from outstanding younger critics. Each essay presents a distinct point of view, and together they constitute a forum of interpretative methods and of the best contemporary ideas on each text.

It is our hope that these volumes will convey the vitality of current critical work in American literature, generate new insights and excitement for students of American literature, and inspire new respect for and new perspectives upon these major literary texts.

University of California, Riverside   EMORY ELLIOTT

List of illustrations

Notes on contributors

Donald Yannella, the volume's editor, is Professor of English, Emeritus, at Rowan University. His books include studies of Emerson and Melville, and he served the Melville Society as an officer for seventeen years, including fifteen as the editor of *Melville Society Extracts*, and filled numerous posts for the Modern Language Association's American Literature Section.

Gail Coffler is Professor of English at Suffolk University in Boston. Her work on Melville and the classics reaches back to her University of Wisconsin dissertation and includes *Melville's Classical Allusions: A Comprehensive Index* and the forthcoming *Melville's Allusions to Religion*, in addition to articles and lectures.

Robert Milder, Professor of English at Washington University in St. Louis, has published widely on Melville and other writers of the American Renaissance. He has edited *Critical Essays on Herman Melville's "Billy Budd, Sailor"* and *Selected Tales* and is currently at work on a book, *Exiled Royalties*, a Melville study.

Larry J. Reynolds, Professor of English and Thomas Franklin Mayo Professor of Liberal Arts at Texas A&M University, is the author of *European Revolutions and the American Literary Renaissance* and co-editor of *New Historical Literary Study*. He has been president of the Nathaniel Hawthorne Society.

John Wenke is Professor of English at Salisbury University in Maryland where he has twice won the university's Distinguished Faculty Award. His books include *J. D. Salinger: A Study of the Short Fiction* and *Melville's Muse: Literary Creation and the Forms of Philosophical Fiction*, as well as numerous chapters, essays, and short stories.

Introduction

When Herman Melville died in 1891, he could hardly have imagined that *Billy Budd* would become one of his most widely read prose fictions; after some five years of working on it, he left the story in a manuscript not to be published until 1924. More than three quarters of a century after its appearance it remains rich for serious general readers, literary critics, legal and military historians, and, of course, college and university students, especially in literature courses (*Billy Budd* is one of the most anthologized of Melville's writings). Others intrigued by this prose fiction are engaged in the ongoing dialogue about the prerogatives and responsibilities of civilized institutions and those in charge of maintaining and preserving their authority and power.

The story Melville was developing evolved into a tale deceptively straightforward in its outlines: Billy Budd, a cheery, popular, and young English merchant sailor – a literal bastard – is impressed into the English Navy to serve aboard a man-of-war, a "ponderously cannoned" and "majestic" battleship. This all takes place "In the time before steamships," as Melville opens his tale, during a 1790s naval battle between the French and English. Once aboard, the "handsome" and enormously popular young sailor immediately arouses the darkest passions of the vessel's chief police officer, John Claggart, the battleship *Bellipotent*'s Master-at-Arms. Billy has left his merchant vessel, the *Rights of Man*, and as millions who have served in the military, he is caught in the grinding gears of institutional procedures and justice. Maligned, falsely accused by Claggart of fomenting a mutiny, Billy retaliates in his fury in perhaps the only manner of which he is capable under the circumstances: He decks him with a punch that kills him. But Melville's tale does not end simply with justice, or what some would argue passes for it, but with justice's miscarriage, or plain injustice. Captain The Honorable Edward Fairfax Vere's agony of decision that leads to Billy's execution perhaps bears the tale's more important meaning. For it is he who effects the handsome sailor's hanging and suffers remorse and guilt for the rest of his short life.

What of the political conditions which create such an impossible situation? Further, what about institutions other than the military which judges Billy's case? Is Billy another historical and perhaps representative victim? (Consider the narrator's recollection of the African sailor and his multicultural mates in the book's second paragraph.) Is he for some readers in the twenty-first century yet another casualty of the insidious, unrelenting, determined and determining forces that doom members of one or another class or race in an array of civilizations and social arrangements to be controlled and crushed by a ruling elite with an eye principally on maintaining its own power? The United States and other countries have long been engaged in the discussion arising from such queries. Was Melville anticipating issues before modern societies, and is this why we read him? Or are such readers interpreting and bending Melville and his work to fit the agenda they wish to promote or at least have discussed? These are just some of the queries and speculations that might be raised by serious readers of Herman Melville's *Billy Budd, Sailor (An Inside Narrative)*.

What were Melville's views on the rights of man, not the ship from which the handsome sailor was impressed, but the fundamental rights and prerogatives asserted and protected so vigorously in the eighteenth century, which had ended fewer than two decades before Melville's birth in 1819? More fundamentally, how concerned was he about the democratic and republican ideas which were articulated in the United States's founding documents such as the *Declaration of Independence*, the *Constitution*, and the *Bill of Rights*? Melville was the grandson of Revolutionary heroes; his mother was from Albany, New York, and of Dutch background, and his father was the son of a Bostonian who participated in that city's notorious Tea Party. The question of just how committed Melville actually was to democratic principles, how much he was one of the so-called "People," the common sailors, has been debated since the Melville Renaissance began in the 1920s when *Billy Budd* was resurrected from the proverbial bread box in the attic.

This man was connected by birth to the privileged, the elite in current jargon. He enjoyed none of the trappings of money and position, however. To get some sense of the quandary faced by the young man of genteel upbringing, one need go no further than the struggles, some of them comic, of the title character in the author's fourth book, *Redburn* (1850). Melville, whose family's financial circumstances were severely reduced by the death of the father when the boy was twelve, shipped out as a merchant seaman at the age of nineteen (the journey was a month-and-a-half round-trip to England) and spent a few years in the South Pacific whale fishery, jumping his original vessel and signing aboard at least one other. This was the personal experience on which *Moby-Dick* (1851) and other early works were based. After some months in Hawaii he joined the United States Navy for the length of a

voyage around Cape Horn and back home to the northeastern
United States. While on the battleship *United States* he met
Jack Chase, the heroic Captain of the Maintop, to whom *Billy
Budd* was dedicated about a half century later. The fictionali-
zed rendering of Melville's own military service is recounted
in his fifth book *White-Jacket* (1850).

So the battleship world young Billy is forced into was not
unknown to his creator. In 1849, Melville crossed the Atlantic
mainly to arrange the English publication of *White-Jacket*,
which among other concerns presented a harshly critical at-
tack on problems in the United States Navy. (This timely
book contributed to lessening the severity of punishments
such as flogging in the US Navy.) But Melville had not lost
his love of the sea, writing in his journal that "Before break-
fast, went up to the mast-head, by way of gymnastics." Two
days later, October 15, he noted with evident pride that "My
occasional feats in the rigging are regarded as a species of
tight-rope dancing."[1] It was only five years and five books
since he had returned from his Pacific adventure, and though
he may have grown at a colossal rate intellectually, he enjoyed showing off – perhaps strutting a bit as many military
men do. His knowledge of the maintopmen enabled him to
understand how elite, daring, and distinguished these men
were compared to the "underlings" on the decks below.[2] The
topmen flew without parachutes in the time before airplanes.

One of the pleasures of Melville's crossing was the company of George J. Adler, a young professor of German at New
York University, with whom Melville seems to have had pleasure passing the time discussing metaphysics, flying high in
the air of abstraction. On the 18th he records that he "Spent the
entire morning in the main-top with" Adler.[3] Here is the new
intellectual Melville pursuing his new interests in the haunts
of his young, old-salt self of a half decade and more earlier.

Such youthful experiences are never forgotten. We know that he was as bothered by flogging, as is evident in *Billy Budd* as it had been in *White-Jacket*. But it appears likely that forty-or-so years later, in the late 1880s, time also may have buffed other aspects of his early adventures in the fleets to a ruddy, glowing nostalgia. The elderly Melville probably enjoyed recalling, even reminiscing about his days on the square-riggers, the setting of the tragic tale he unfolded.

Discipline on the military vessel was different from that on board ships in the private fleets. At the time Melville was in the Pacific from 1841 to 1844, his cousin Guert Gansevoort sat on the court which condemned to death three alleged mutineers, including Philip Spencer, the son of Secretary of War John C. Spencer. The case was a major event and was even mentioned occasionally in the public press when he was writing *Billy Budd*; it was no doubt one of the streams flowing into Melville's meditation on Billy and those he touches and who touch him.[4]

The *Billy Budd* genetic text reveals just how much Melville pondered the situation about which he was writing: how he kept returning to it, modifying it, shifting and refining character portraits, thematic emphases, bringing the tale's actors out from the shadows and returning them there. Which brings us to the question of what specifically in a word or few Melville was trying to say. What was the truth he was trying to convey?

The short answer is that we do not know. As long as a reader is not intent on bending or warping the author's text to accommodate an ideological position, for example, at the expense of fathoming the statement the author is trying to make, then a serious search for the writer's meaning can take place. This is what professional literary critics and serious amateurs do, or should do, as a matter of course when engaging a text. Granted, disagreements will occur due to one or another reader's disposition or predilections. But the problem of finding the author's meaning is compounded by a writer such as Melville. For he was a philosophical skeptic.[5]

To begin addressing ourselves to this and related issues, we must first acknowledge his skepticism, his wariness of certainty, assumed truth, or, to use the philosophical term, certitude. One might point to numerous passages in his collected writings to demonstrate this. His third prose work, *Mardi* (1849) and his long poem *Clarel* (1876) are often viewed as speculations about truth-seeking. In the former, which Melville began a few years after making his smashing debut as a serious and popular New York author, he began with the formula he used in *Typee* (1846) and *Omoo* (1847) to earn some celebrity with a tasteful reading public. But after *Mardi*'s opening chapters which promised yet another South Seas adventure, Melville swamped his volume by testing the store of knowledge he had managed to gain in the few short years since he had returned from his Pacific adventure. Political, social, aesthetic observations, for instance, were packed aboard; philosophical and theological speculation and rumination, probably intended to make the volume fly higher in the minds of his audience, turned to ballast. The volume sank – failed. Yet Melville demonstrated how much he was learning, how intensely he was reading, reflecting, and writing. In short, he revealed how powerful an intellectual he had become during the several years that had passed since his return from the Pacific.

Melville's intellectualism, his continuing quest for ideas, simply made the possibilities of truth too elusive for him – or any intelligent person for that matter – to settle on a position. On his way to the Holy Land, Melville visited Nathaniel Hawthorne in England; the latter noted in his journal that evening, November 12, 1856: "Melville, as he always does, began to reason of Providence and futurity, and of everything that lies beyond human ken, and he informed me that he had 'pretty much made up his mind to be annihilated;' but he does not seem to rest in that anticipation; and, I think, will never rest until he gets hold of a definite belief. It is strange how he persists – and has persisted ever since I knew him, and probably long before – in wandering to and fro over these deserts. . . . He can neither believe, nor be comfortable in his unbelief; and he is too honest and courageous not to try to do one or the other. If he were a religious man, he would be one of the most truly religious and reverential; he has a very high and noble nature, and better worth immortality than most of us."[6]

Two passages in *Moby-Dick*, the centerpiece of the Melville canon, make the point. Ishmael, the book's narrator, provides an analogy about the virtually nonexistent possibilities for a human to achieve truth. In a rather manic passage Ishmael, having just read the wall tablets in the Seamen's Bethel commemorating some of those lost in the whale fishery, realizes the enormous danger he faces. In bursts of almost hysterical fear, sarcasm, fatalistic resignation, he says at the end of Chapter 7: "Yes, there is death in this business of whaling – a speechlessly quick chaotic bundling of a man into Eternity. But what then? Methinks we have hugely mistaken this matter of Life and Death. Methinks that what they call my shadow here on earth is my true substance. Methinks that in looking at things spiritual, we are too much like oysters observing the sun through water, and thinking that water the thinnest of air."[7] The assertion signals Ishmael's growing philosophical skepticism and his increasing caution, ambiguity, reluctance, even refusal, to make commitments. He alone survives the mad quest after the white whale; the rest of the crew are killed. Ishmael may give himself to Ahab's obsession near the start of the voyage, but withdraws into a safer "Ifs eternally" attitude, a position more in keeping with Melville's own tentative, cautious philosophical view.

Some readers argue that forty years later in *Billy Budd* Melville would raise the same sort of doubts about Claggart and Vere's monomaniacal behavior in handling the case of the handsome sailor, paralleling their pursuits with Ahab's quest after the white whale.

In a key passage in which the certitudes, among other possibilities, are being pondered, Ishmael describes humanity's life cycle: "There is no steady unretracing progress in this life; we do not advance through fixed gradations, and at the last one pause: – through infancy's unconscious spell, boyhood's thoughtless faith, adolescence doubt (the common doom), then skepticism, then disbelief, resting at last in manhood's pondering repose of If. But once gone through, we trace the round again; and are infants, boys, and men, and Ifs eternally."[8]

One might even pursue the question as it is approached by pondering the very name of the narrator in Melville's sixth long fiction. The opening line is so memorable it entered the popular culture some seventy-five years ago during the beginning of the Melville Renaissance; it reads, "Call me Ishmael." We are invited, or allowed, to call him by the name of the biblical wanderer, but it is not necessarily his name. Wandering, an elusive identity, and skepticism are linked and compressed nicely in the biblical allusion to Ishmael which Melville's contemporaries would have caught immediately. The *Billy Budd* narrator's not having a name is probably not without significance.

So ascertaining the statement or "message" Melville is conveying in his writing is a matter of debate among serious readers. There are no simple, reductive answers, even to apparently simple queries such as the meaning of *the* statement

Melville is making in *Billy Budd*. His canon is suffused by ambiguous statements, hints, sly pokes in the readers' ribs about the search for truth. One might even suggest that as with many people as they age, Melville became less sure of any verities, however many or few he had ever embraced, even tentatively. Hawthorne, who first met him in 1850, made his 1856 journal comments about his friend's intellectual wanderings more than thirty years before Melville wrote *Billy Budd*.

For the impatient or reductive person this can make reading Melville frustrating. This is especially true in periods of cultural tension during which societies are polarized or fractured. In such times, emotions run high, passions rage, and people look to their leaders for direct, simple answers and solutions, easily comprehended and readily assented to and effected. In Melville's lifetime there were issues such as "Manifest Destiny" played out, for example, in the Mexican War of the late 1840s. Melville publicly attacked it in his satirical essays on Zachary Taylor, at the time a general and soon to become President of the United States.[9] Among the other tensions, one might consider issues of public debate such as slavery, abolition, Southern secession, and the countless deeply emotional questions Melville and his contemporaries faced in the expansive post-Civil War boom – Twain's gilded age. In the twentieth century Melville's voice spoke eloquently to cultural shocks such as the Vietnam conflict and all the attendant issues bursting from the turbulent 1960s which witnessed questionings of fundamental values, beliefs, mores that will continue to vex, even torment, cultures for decades to come.

The authors of the new essays presented here are writing in the serious tradition of inquiry about Melville's meanings that has been in progress for almost a century. The center of discussion during seventy-five of those years has been in colleges and universities, principally in the United States but also wherever American literature has been and is being read.

To use one of Melville's more widely familiar analogies, drawn from the whale fishery, what the present authors and others are engaged in is a cutting into the *Billy Budd* text, seeking as Ahab's crew did a "little lower layer." Whalers sliced ever deeper into their prey to retrieve its oil and other valuable products; in search of meaning critical crews carve deeper and deeper into the text's body. And as already suggested, what they discover is varied.

Perhaps Merton M. Sealts, Jr., the late dean of *Billy Budd* studies, said it best: "But how to read that final story, as its narrator pointedly declares, 'everyone must determine for himself,' and it is tempting to say as many interpretations have been advanced as there have been readers and critics."[10]

The contributors present a variety of interest, knowledge, methodologies, and critical postures, each intended to bring forth and illuminate the richness buried in Melville's contemplation of the issues to which he was addressing himself. It is a dozen years since it was suggested that "Among the areas most promising for future investigation are Melville's late reading, his response to contemporary social and political developments, his interest in the arts and in myth."[11] These accurately anticipated the focus of some of the more important recent Melville criticism. But before turning to the essays collected here, a review of the book's critical history is in order.

Since *Billy Budd*'s posthumous appearance, it has gone through stages of interpretation, some clearly fashions or even trends, by professionals and general readers.[12]

When first published in the 1920s, *Billy Budd* was interpreted on the obvious level of allegory between good and evil; then as interest turned to Melville's life as "spiritual autobiography," the question arose about whether the text was the author's "last will and testament," his summing up or arriving at a conclusion in his old age about the large philosophical and theological questions he had been pondering over a lifetime. Some saw the tale as a "testament of acceptance" of the human lot; others interpreted it as a rejection of humanity's fate, in effect a condemnation of inhumane behavior such as Vere's which leads to Billy's tragic hanging.

During the mid-century period the reigning New Critics insisted we focus on texts and eschew what they saw as extraneous or irrelevant interpretive factors such as social, political, biographical, and other concerns. Consider the work as artifact. There was a flurry of Ironist interpretations, sophisticated close readings which insisted, for example, that Billy's last words, "God bless Captain Vere," be understood as ironic; opponents asked how and why this innocent and naive, but nevertheless illiterate young man, would be capable of such sophisticated intellectual cleverness at the moment his life was about to be taken, in large measure because of Vere's actions. Past mid-century, social and political upheavals (especially in the 1960s on the campuses) provided the emotionally charged atmosphere in which Billy was seen as a precursor of the thousands of young troops being shipped to southeast Asia to wage the hot war which tore apart many societies in the United States and in Europe. Opposing the defenders of the "crucified" Billy were Vere's champions who argued for the necessity of the captain's maintaining order at a critical time when the necessary military discipline and his and other commanders' authority might be eroded and collapse into chaos.

So the cultural dialogue continues in periods of emotional public debate on issues such as armed conflict and the quest for human or civil rights in autocratic states with long histories of authoritarian control of the masses, the "people," as they were designated aboard naval vessels such as the *Bellipotent*. And in the past twenty-five years or so there has emerged a stream of politically charged readings, some of them sophisticated, in the frameworks established by post-modernist, post-structuralist "critical theory"; many have unblushingly promoted political and social agendas, ideological positions – in short made Melville's text fit their own purposes, frequently with an intensity greater than their predecessors'.[13] The situation has been nicely characterized: "the warring factions of acceptance and resistance critics, straight readers and ironists, conservatives and progressives, subsume an ambiguous text to their characteristic ways of ordering the world and assigning value."[14]

This subjectivism is what the scholars in this collection seek to avoid. What they are offering are contributions that point to strategies that serious readers might consider in trying to ascertain what Melville himself was trying to communicate or at least explore in his last, unfinished work: the pregnant and potent, large questions which thinking human beings confront.

The political and social implications of *Billy Budd* have dominated discussions among general readers as well as scholars in the several decades since the so-called New Criticism began to wane and presumably dissolve, though it has done so only slowly and grudgingly. Yet no matter how much the conversation among serious readers might center on political and social commentary, such as the obvious homoerotic resonances, the *literary artifact* – which is after all what the tale of the handsome sailor is – must be judged, at least partially, on its aesthetic merit. What has all too often been lost by activist modern readers is that Melville was not an activist, nor was he a social, political, or behavioral scientist. He was a *literary artist* composing intellectually charged fiction and poetry about cultural issues which are markedly different from all but a handful of commentaries and treatises published by "soft" scientists.

Melville published only poetry after the 1857 appearance of his prose fiction, *The Confidence-Man*. But at his best, beginning with *Typee*, he displayed a remarkable talent for poetic prose, especially if treating a subject which captured his artistic imagination. This continued to be true near the end of his life.

Consider the language in the passage at the end of Chapter 25, the scene where Billy is hanged. Billy speaks, "God bless Captain Vere!" and the "ship's populace," the people whose ranks Melville himself had once been part of, "with one voice from alow and aloft" sound "a resonant sympathetic echo" of Billy's virtual benediction. Vere "either through self-control or a sort of momentary paralysis induced by emotional shock, stood erect as a musket in the ship-armorer's rack"; this unbending resolve, somewhat threatening, in this climactic scene, is counterpointed by the narrator's next words which open a new paragraph: "The hull, deliberately recovering from the periodic roll to leeward, was just regaining an even keel when the last signal, a preconcerted dumb one, was given," and "Billy ascended; and, ascending, took the full rose of the dawn."

The silence, the command's rigidity, the potential threat in that "wedged mass of upturned faces" who witness the hanging provide a dumb show, a pantomime. The tragedy is set not upon a proscenium stage (where Benjamin Britten's operatic adaptation is mounted) but on a heaving, rolling man-of-war, as in Peter Ustinov's film adaptation. Melville's language suggests the ship-of-the-line's ponderous weight simply with the long, low, drawn-out "r" sound in all words but the article and one preposition: "deliberately recovering from the periodic roll to leeward." And his use of polysyllabic words which roll off the tongue when spoken further enhances the description of the events. Yet somewhat surprisingly, "In the pinioned figure," the hanged handsome sailor, "no motion was apparent. . . ." And Melville concludes the chapter on a bass note, the only language tone appropriate for the denouement of this part: no motion, "none save that created by the slow roll of the hull in moderate weather, so majestic in a great ship ponderously cannoned." The polysyllables' elongated sounds work in the passage above; here, the short words, even monosyllables, equally drawn out, capture the tragedy's heaviness: "no motion," "slow, roll of the hull," "so majestic in a great ship ponderously cannoned."[15]

The draft's stages suggest an old Melville worrying and fretting over the slow growth of the tale that his narrator was unfolding,[16] but it also reveals an artist crafting the materials of his medium with as much care and success as the painter's strategies with colors and brush strokes, the sculptor's manipulating chiselings and welds, the composer's planning sound sequences. Here muting verbal sound amplifies and suggests sense and meaning, and is integral to the passage's success. In these slightly more than four paragraphs, Melville was writing as well, though more slowly, as he had in passages of the great prose fictions, including *Moby-Dick*, about forty years earlier; then he was in prime writing condition and could work long hours churning out the work. Near the end of his life it took longer; he was more deliberate and no doubt more reflective, cautious, and probing.

Many passages in the *Billy Budd* reading text are dense and packed, perhaps difficult to comprehend on a quick first read. Melville's worrying over the unfolding tale was perhaps due to his struggling with the crafting of his vehicle, the poetic-prose tale, as he was contemplating the unfolding statement, the lower layers he was reaching. There were probably family-related issues at deep layers which he had been confronting for twenty years and more: the suicide of his eighteen-year-old son Malcolm and all the questions and pain it raised about authority and patriarchy, fathers and sons – Malcolm and Billy, Melville and Vere, and the echoes of the patriarchal tradition.[17]

He was an artist and an intellectual and not least a man making what he perhaps came to realize might be his last statement. No light matter for an elderly intellectual in failing health.

Each contributor to this volume sees Melville from his or her own perspective. While Larry J. Reynolds has long been exploring how nineteenth-century political and social dynamics initiated and formed, in some way affected, literary response, Gail Coffler provides a complementary approach by offering her insight into mythology and the histories of the classical world and Judaeo-Christian civilization. Robert Milder pursues his ongoing interest in Melville's later writing, not only *Billy Budd* but the late poetry. And John Wenke offers a close reading of Melville's last fiction, relying on the reading text qualified by considerations of the genetic text, an approach encouraged by Hayford and Sealts in their 1962 edition.[18]

These contributors bring serious scholarship to their explorations and analyses; no one pursues the trendy, the academically fashionable, no one promotes ideological agendas. These essays are aimed at opening the possibilities of Melville's concerns and artistry in *Billy Budd*.

The social and political background Reynolds provides serves as a realistic backdrop for comprehending the worldly experience in which *Billy Budd* is grounded. However patrician Melville's family was, the death of his father when Herman was twelve plunged the family into near poverty and rendered them dependent on wealthy relatives such as Peter Gansevoort, his mother Maria's brother. Melville, as we have seen, had actual experience in the merchant, whaling, and naval fleets before he was twenty-five. And financial necessity forced him into the customs service where he was on the docks and in the holds inspecting ships. Starting in his late forties, he served for nineteen years until 1885 when he earned a pension,[19] a year before the infamous Haymarket debacle, one of the more memorable labor upheavals of the time. Melville knew the world of work, and he was fully conversant with the changing ethnic and political faces of New York City where he lived the last twenty-eight years of his life. Reynolds's explorations of these volatile times and contexts provide readers with a sense of how much the circumstances of contemporary life affected Melville and, as Reynolds suggests, helped form certain layers of meaning for his last prose fiction. His essay is provocative for modern readers when issues of democracy, the rights of ordinary working people, continue to collide with the interests of established elites. We are probably as polarized as many were in Melville's own period, not only in the United States but in Europe, virtually the entire world. The industrial revolution bred labor problems which intensified throughout Melville's life and will continue well beyond ours.

Coffler considers Melville's knowledge and use of classical and biblical literature and explores mythopoetic resonances in his last fiction. After addressing herself to what she asserts are clear reflections of classical heroes such as Alexander, Achilles, Hercules, she follows scholars such as Nathalia Wright[20] and turns her attention to the Judaeo-Christian tradition which was the foundation of religious belief in the nineteenth-century West, the culture which Melville inherited and inhabited. Using the thinking of the enormously influential and provocative Matthew Arnold, she categorizes and discusses the major characters in *Billy Budd* — the handsome sailor himself, of course, and Vere, as well as Claggart. Further, she draws certain parallels between Melville's last tale and the fiction which brought his career as a professional literary man to an end, *The Confidence-Man*, published only eleven years after he made his debut with *Typee* in 1846. And as do others in this collection she confronts the issue of Melville's philosophical skepticism.

Milder's study of the connections between *Billy Budd* and the contemporaneous "Weeds and Wildings" poetry collection is one of a series of studies in which he is engaged with an eye toward comprehending the meaning, depth, and value of these all-too-often neglected poems. After the appearance of *The Confidence-Man*, Melville turned his talents toward poetry, beginning with the Civil War collection *Battle Pieces* (1867), the long poem *Clarel* (1876) set in the Holy Land, and the small, privately printed collection of his old age, *John Marr and Other Sailors* (1888) which included the Billy poem that became the foundation of *Billy Budd*. In his exploration of a Melville at last with enough leisure to think and write pieces such as *Billy Budd* and "Weeds and Wildings" without the pressure of earning the family's daily bread, Milder demonstrates how the works complement each other and reveal the author's disciplined and penetrating mind. More tempered perhaps by age and experience, and the wisdom they provide, Melville's intellect was as powerful as ever, if more nuanced and subtle.

Wenke's essay concludes the collection principally because it addresses several major concerns readers of the story have, and because in its concentration on the Hayford and Sealts genetic text, as well as on their reading text, it provides a deep insight into the problems of what Wenke describes as only a "nearly finished" work. He also offers a methodology which future readers might employ to advantage.

Wenke's is the first of a few essays he has composed on Melville's thought and *Billy Budd* in which he interprets the tale by using the Hayford and Sealts genetic text. It has been studied and used to interpretive advantage only occasionally in the almost forty years since it has been available. The genetic text is also utilized by the others in this volume.

Wenke also concentrates on the reliability of the story's narrator. He is, after all – as in so many modern renderings as well as those of Melville's contemporaries such as Poe and James, to mention just two – the filter through which we know what we do about the events. As Wenke in effect says, the issue probably has less to do with narrative experimentation for Melville at this late point in his career than it does with the question of skepticism: the narrator is an equivocator. As has been suggested above, Ishmael, the filter through whom we hear the story of the white whale, is a teller who must be considered if readers are to have any reasonable hope of arriving at an approximation of Melville's reality in *Moby-Dick*. And so it is with the lawyer/narrator who tells us what we know of that other memorable character, Bartleby, scrivener and mystery man.

This should be encouraging for readers returning to *Billy Budd* as well as for initiates. Not only is there a host of new queries to be asked, but if the genetic text is employed as it should be, the interpretive yield should bring us to progressively lower layers of contemplation, understanding, and speculation.

As noted in 1989 the then "present debate has run its course and consists largely of a restatement of old positions in new or not-so-new vocabularies."[21] Little has changed in the past dozen years. The contributors here are offering a series of beginnings which will enliven and enrich the discussion of *Billy Budd*. And in that process, we will achieve an even deeper appreciation of this brilliant author's penetrating intellect and art. That intelligence, after all, is what separated – perhaps alienated – him from his own society and is among the reasons that have made him so popular since he first began to emerge as an intellectual and artist to be reckoned with in the modern world.

NOTES

1 Herman Melville, *Journals*, ed. Howard C. Horsford and Lynn Horth (Evanston and Chicago: Northwestern University Press and The Newberry Library, 1989), pp. 5, 7.

2 "Notes and Commentary," in Herman Melville, *Billy Budd, Sailor (An Inside Narrative)*, ed. Harrison Hayford and Merton M. Sealts, Jr. (University of Chicago Press, 1962), pp. 137, 139–40, 156–57.

3 *Journals*, 8 and 251.

4 Hayford and Sealts, "Editors' Introd.," 30.

5 Hayford and Sealts, "Editors' Introd.," 38–39.

6 Jay Leyda, *The Melville Log* (New York: Gordion, 1969), 2, 529.

7 Herman Melville, *Moby-Dick, or the Whale*, ed. Harrison Hayford, Hershel Parker, and G. Thomas Tanselle (Evanston and Chicago: Northwestern University Press and The Newberry Library, 1988), p. 37.

8 *Moby-Dick*, 492. The editors of the Northwestern/Newberry edition (N/N) attribute this speech to Ahab on the dubious basis of the "structure of the chapter" (901), contradicting Hayford and Parker's assigning it to Ishmael in their Norton Critical Edition.

This "Ifs eternally" passage has long been attributed to Ishmael and articulates a flexibility of position in keeping with his posture throughout the book, in contrast to Ahab who is sure and inflexible.

9 Herman Melville, *The Piazza Tales and Other Prose Pieces*, ed. Harrison Hayford, Alma A. MacDougall, and G. Thomas Tanselle (Evanston and Chicago: Northwestern University Press and The Newberry Library, 1987), pp. 212–29.

10 Merton M. Sealts, Jr., "Innocence and Infamy: *Billy Budd, Sailor*," in John Bryant. *A Companion to Melville Studies* (New York: Greenwood, 1986), 417.

11 Robert Milder, "Introd.," *Critical Essays on Melville's Billy Budd, Sailor* (Boston, Mass.: G.K. Hall, 1989), 15.

12 Sealts, "Innocence and Infamy," 421–24; see also Hayford and Sealts, "Editors' Introd.," 25–27, and Milder, "Introd.," 3–18. These and the commentaries and selections in the several other collections of critical statements noted in the bibliography and its headnote provide summary introductions to the critical history. Milder's is especially valuable because his selection is representative and his introduction places the essays reprinted in context.

13 Eve Kosofsky Sedgwick, *Epistemology of the Closet* (Berkeley and Los Angeles: University of California Press, 1990), 91–131, offers a startling appraisal. See also Barbara Johnson, *The Critical Difference: Essays in the Contemporary Rhetoric of Reading* (Baltimore: The Johns Hopkins University Press, 1980), 79–109, 151–52.

14 Milder, "Introd.": 11.

15 *Billy Budd*, 121–22.

16 Hayford and Sealts, "Notes and Commentary," 192, discuss the progress of Melville's alterations in the genetic text.

17 Hennig Cohen and Donald Yannella, *Herman Melville's Malcolm Letter: "Man's Final Lore"* (New York: Fordham University Press and The New York Public Library, 1992), 41 and 73. This study concerns Melville's family background and life and the effect these traditions had on him, his thought, and his writing.

18 They hoped for "new perspectives, for criticism as well as scholarship, afforded by the complete transcription of the manuscript and our detailed analysis of its genesis and development." Hayford and Sealts, "Editors' Introd.," 27.

19 Stanton Garner, "Melville in the Custom House, 1881–82: A Rustic Beauty among the High-Born Dames of Court," *Melville Society Extracts* 35 (September 1978), 12–14.

20 Nathalia Wright, *Melville's Use of the Bible* (Durham, N.C.: Duke University Press, 1949), passim.

21 Milder, "Introd.," 18.

Billy Budd *and American labor unrest: the case for striking back*

Larry J. Reynolds

> It seems an inconsistency to assert unconditional democracy in all things, and yet confess a dislike to all mankind – in the mass. But not so.
>
> — MELVILLE, Letter to Nathaniel Hawthorne (June 1851)[1]

"The times are revolutionary," declared John Swinton, the former editor of the *New York Sun*,[2] and his fellow New Yorker Herman Melville surely agreed, for the times were the mid-1880s and the United States was experiencing one of the most sustained periods of violent labor unrest in its history. The French revolution of 1871 marked the beginning of three decades of bitter class struggle in America as workers, influenced by the worldwide socialist movement, struck for better wages, shorter hours, and improved working conditions. The vast influx of eight million immigrants into the United States during 1870–90 led to a cycle of wage-cutting, union organization, strikes, and reaction. During the peak years of upheaval, 1877, 1886, and 1892–93, tens of thousands of strikes, involving hundreds of thousands of workers, occurred in a number of industries across the country.[3] Owners, employers, and their representatives in city, state, and federal governments called the strikes "insurrections," linked them to the "Paris Commune," and denounced the strikers as "anarchists," "communists," "Reds," "foreign agitators," and "bomb-throwers." Meanwhile, urban newspapers and magazines depicted union workers as dark, unshaven men arriving from abroad, armed with swords, bombs, rifles, and cannon.⁴ As Melville developed his narrative about what befell Billy Budd during the year of "the Great Mutiny," he did so in a society anxious about violence, eager for order, and willing to use armed force to impose it. Did Melville concern himself with these issues? Does *Billy Budd* incorporate his response to them? This essay will suggest some provisional answers to these questions by looking at *Billy Budd* within the contexts of the 1880s and of Melville's career. The thesis it will advance is that *Billy Budd* becomes a site – charged by contemporary events – for Melville to revisit and review the issues of democracy and authority, revolution and reform, violence and order, which had long concerned him, and to dramatize the value and cost of a conservative stance toward them.

I

Despite the nostalgia that permeates *John Marr and Other Sailors* (1888), the contemporary strikes and riots that unsettled America surely caught Melville's attention. Current events had always interested him, and in the last decades of his life, he had ample opportunity to follow them. He lived in the country's largest city; he read its papers; he walked its streets. From 1866 to 1885, he was a district inspector of customs in New York City, working first along the North River waterfront at 207 West Street, then at 62 Harrison Street (which was nearer his home at 104 East 26th Street), and finally at 76th Street and the East River. As he began *Billy Budd* early in 1886 by writing the prose headnote to the ballad "Billy in the Darbies," labor unrest broke out near at hand. In March 1886 the city was disrupted by a series of violent street car strikes, which lead to massive police action against the strikers (see Figure 1.1). During the first week of March, New York

Figure 1 T. De Thulstrup, *The Street Railroad Strike in New York — The Police Opening the Way for a Horsecar.*

horse-car drivers and conductors tied up every major road in the city, from the Battery to East 34th Street. After attempts to run a car through Grand Street failed when strikers blocked the tracks with lumber, bricks, barrels, and cobble-stones, city officials called out the police and 750 of them escorted the same car along its route, encountering opposition from workers and their sympathizers. At Eldrige Street, when a baggage truck was overturned to block the way, the police charged the crowd, and according to one report, "With wild cries of alarm the crowd scattered in all directions, a few badly clubbed, some injured by being trampled upon, while show windows were smashed, and hats and bonnets were strewn on the street as the result of the fray."[5] The striking drivers and the railroad company reached an agreement the following day, yet the "labor agitation," as it was called, persisted in the months that followed.

On May 4, 1886, a more deadly and explosive confrontation between workers and police occurred in Chicago at Haymarket Square, which received widespread newspaper coverage and led to the most sensational trial of the decade. On May 3, strikers had fought with scabs at the McCormick Harvester Company, and the Chicago police fired on the strikers, killing four men and wounding many more. In protest, some 3,000 people gathered in Haymarket Square the next evening and listened to speeches condemning the police and their actions. As the crowd was breaking up, the police moved in with raised clubs. A dynamite bomb exploded in their midst, and they opened fire on the crowd. Six policemen were killed by the bomb, and some fifty were injured; several workers were killed by the police and at least 200 were wounded.[6] Public outrage and blame about this bloodshed were directed toward the anarchists who had spoken out on behalf of the strike. A widely circulated illustration in *Harper's Weekly* dramatized the perceived ties between the anarchists and the violence (see Figure 1.2), as speaker and bomb mirror one another in the picture's horizontal composition.

After the bombing, the Chicago police raided meeting halls, printing offices, and private homes, arrested hundreds of workers, and charged eight leading anarchists with murder. Although no evidence linked them directly to the bombing, the eight men were accused of having incited the unknown bomb-thrower. A few prominent citizens, such as William Dean Howells, spoke out on their behalf, but public opinion ran strongly against them. The majority view was expressed by the owner of a Chicago clothing firm who declared, "No, I don't consider these people to have been found guilty of any offense, *but they must be hanged . . . the labor movement must be crushed* !"[7]

In the wake of the Haymarket bombing, New York and other cities witnessed judicial reaction. As Philip Foner has explained, "the Police and the courts were assigned an important role in the employers' counter-offensive; police activity was matched by judicial tyranny. Arrests and imprisonment of strikers and boycotters on the spurious charge of 'conspiracy' occurred all over the country".[8] An editorial in *Harper's Weekly* entitled "The Anarchists at Chicago" rationalized the contemporary legal severity by declaring, "Anarchists who justify and counsel murder as necessary to the overthrow of society, when murder begins in consequence of that incitement, cannot be held guiltless. . . . it is the welfare of society and the security of liberty under law which alone should determine the kind and degree of the penalty!"[9] With even less moderation, an editorial in the November 25 *New York Times* called the anarchists "a gang of villains" and "mad dogs," and then declared: "In such a case even Judges may be expected to be guided by a sense of stern justice, and to regard it as

Figure 2 T. De Thulstrup, *The Anarchist Riot in Chicago — A Dynamite Bomb Exploding Among the Police.*

desirable that the wretched brood should be exterminated."[10]
Amidst such hostility, the anarchists were found guilty, and
seven were sentenced to death. Governor Oglesby commuted
the sentences of two to life imprisonment; one committed
suicide in his cell, and on November 11, 1887 four of them
were hanged. "Law and order must be maintained when revolution threatens," declared the author of an article entitled
"The Lesson of Chicago."[11] The unfairness of the trial did not
dawn on most Americans until the twentieth century, and
when Illinois Govenor John Peter Altgeld issued his famous
pardon on June 26, 1893, declaring the defendants completely
innnocent victims of a biased judge and packed juries, he became one of the most reviled men in America.[12]

The issues of conspiracy, rebellion, armed force, and repression figure prominently in *Billy Budd*, of course, and seem
clearly linked to the contemporary scene. "The similarities of
historical moment – of mass unrest and challenges to authority,
of issues brought to law and settled by authorized force –
resound too insistently to be ignored," as Alan Trachtenberg
has pointed out.[13] Moreover, distinctive features of the
Haymarket affair – the harsh justice, the scapegoating, the
death by hanging – have persuaded several critics that this
event served as a particular source for Melville's narrative.[14]
Like the Haymarket defendants, Billy is an innocent man
hung to preserve order during a time of revolutionary strife.
Whether like them he is also the victim of a biased judge and
unfair trial, however, remains an open question.[15] Critical
controversy has long surrounded Melville's authority figure,
Captain Vere.

On the one hand, one can argue that Vere prejudges the
case against Billy, uses irregular proceedings to convict him,
and then executes him in a gross miscarriage of justice. On the
other, one can argue that Vere, though filled with compassion

for Billy, acts with a heroic presence of mind during a crisis, preserving the social order by an act of stern yet necessary justice. Milton Stern has been the most prominent advocate for this second view, and he has persuasively argued that "in *Billy Budd*, with many modifications and exceptions, with anger and depression, Melville is making a tortured choice for conservatism."[16] Vere's conservative rationale for hanging Billy, of course, is that it will silence and tame the sailors, who otherwise will take the captain's inaction as a sign of weakness and an excuse to rebel. "You know what sailors are," Vere says, in response to the Sailing Master's suggestion of clemency. "Will they not revert to the recent outbreak at the Nore? Ay. They know the well-founded alarm – the panic it struck throughout England. Your clement sentence they would account pusillanimous. They would think that we flinch, that we are afraid of them – afraid of practising a lawful rigor singularly demanded at this juncture, lest it should provoke new troubles."[17] Although a number of critics have perceived irony at work here, Melville's earlier treatments of revolutionary action suggest that he linked it with anarchy and bloodshed. In other words, he shared Vere's conviction that "with mankind, forms, measured forms are everything" (128), and he applied this to disruptions at home and abroad throughout his life.

II

Melville's sociopolitical views were complex and at times self-contradictory, for they involved an "unconditional democracy" based on a faith in man in the ideal and a conservative elitism based on distrust for the mass of mankind.[18] Melville's democracy figures prominently in *Billy Budd*, at times, especially in the portrayal of Billy as an ideal common sailor, "an angel of God" (101), visually transfigured like Christ. Nevertheless, his conservatism also informs the novel, especially in the positive portrayal of Vere as a humane and rational captain struggling to do what is right in a world that is wrong. In many respects the novel dramatizes the dilemma posed in the famous "The Journey and the Pamphlet" chapter of *Pierre* (1852), where Melville elaborates upon the difficulties of reconciling celestial (chronometrical) time with terrestrial (horological) time – Heaven and Earth, the Ideal and the Actual. Does one execute a morally innocent man in order to secure the welfare of mankind? Only in a fallen world, Melville suggests, does such a question arise, yet we live in a fallen world.

Melville had served as a common sailor himself aboard five different ships during 1839–44, and in his early writings, *White-Jacket* (1850) especially, he vigorously affirms the inherent dignity and equality of the common sailors and castigates naval officers who abuse their authority and deny the sailors their basic human rights. Nevertheless, he also describes the depravity and ignorance of the "people," and shows disdain toward them. He reserves his highest regard for grand and glowing individuals, such as Jack Chase, who possess superior social, moral, and intellectual gifts. In *Moby-Dick* (1851), the two sides of Melville's sociopolitical thought come to the fore when Ishmael declares, "take high abstracted man alone; and he seems a wonder, a grandeur, and a woe. But . . . take mankind in mass, and for the most part, they seem a mob of unnecessary duplicates."[19]

For Melville, the dark side of mankind in the mass surfaced most noticeably and frighteningly during riots, mutinies, rebellions, and revolutions. He had been fascinated by popular violence for many years, and like most of his countrymen, he reacted negatively to it, even when oppression and injustice were clearly its cause. *Moby-Dick* can be read as his most emotional treatment of revolutionary action (the red flag of revolt signals Ahab's radicalism), while *Billy Budd* is his most sustained analysis of the difficulties inherent in suppressing such action. During his early career, scenes from the French Revolution of 1789 were fresh in his mind, thanks to stories heard in his youth, from his Uncle Thomas especially. The Revolution possessed for him and his contemporaries an immediacy and reality that have been lost in the twentieth century due to the passage of time. The French revolutions of 1848 and 1871 reawakened memories of the "Reign of Terror" and provided their own dramas of violence and bloodshed that Melville and other Americans found appalling.[20]

The political allegory he added to *Mardi* (1849) in response to the European revolutions of 1848 contains an explicit anticipation of the treatment of French and English radicalism in *Billy Budd*. When the Mardian travellers approach Franko (France) in the earlier work, they see a violent eruption accompanied by the din of warfare, showers of embers, and whirling blasts. "The fiery storm from Franko, kindled new flames in the distant valleys of Porpheero [Europe]," Melville writes, "while driven over from Verdanna came frantic shouts, and direful jubilees. Upon Dominora [England] a baleful glare was resting." Media, the king, cries, "See! how the flames blow over upon Dominora!" while the philosopher Babbalanja answers, "Yet the fires they kindle there are soon extinguished. No, no; Dominora ne'er can burn with Franko's fires; only those of her own kindling may consume her."[21] In *Billy Budd*, Melville reuses this fire imagery as he describes the Nore mutiny: "Reasonable discontent growing out of practical grievances in the fleet had been ignited into irrational combustion as by live cinders blown across the Channel from France in flames" (54).

The distinction between "reasonable discontent" and "irrational combustion" made in both cases points to a key aspect of Melville's sociopolitical thought. For him, practical grievances and reasonable discontent needed to be addressed through reform; when they burst into "irrational combustion" or revolution, his sympathy turned to antipathy. His support for reform never developed into support for revolution; rather, he urged readers to value existential reality over abstract principles when it came to the revolutionary trinity of *liberté, egalité,* and *fraternité.* In *Mardi,* Melville comments upon the Paris workers' revolt of June 1849 by introducing a mysterious scroll that expresses a number of Burkean reflections on recent events. This scroll asserts, "Better, on all hands that peace should rule with a scepter, than the tribunes of the people should brandish their broadswords. Better be the subject of a king, upright and just; than a freeman in Franko, with the executioner's ax at every corner" (527). Violence brings only harm the scroll maintains: although "great reforms, of a verity, be needed; nowhere are bloody revolutions required. Though it be the most certain of remedies, no prudent invalid opens his veins, to let out his disease with his life" (529). The travelers in *Mardi* accuse one another of being the scroll's author, but Melville terms it "a Voice from the Gods" (523).

The Civil War, as observed, seemed a bloody revolution in the making to many Americans, and Melville offered conservative reflections upon it in his *Battle-Pieces and Aspects of the War* (1866). In several of his poems, he expresses a Vere-like commitment to form and law as he indicts the forces of rebellion. "Dupont's Round Fight," for example, which treats the battle fought at Port Royal Sound, South Carolina, on November 7, 1861, ends with the declaration:

> The rebel at Port Royal felt
>   The Unity overawe,
>   And rued the spell. A type was here,
>   And victory of LAW.[22]

A comparable poem, "The House-Top," treats the New York Draft Riots of 1863 and reveals a similar conservative commitment to law and order. Here the masses give voice to "the Atheist roar of riot," and illuminate themselves by "red Arson," until the militia, "wise Draco," arrives and restores order. The thrust of the poem is that the author's countrymen are unaware of the challenge to democratic ideals implied in their approval of armed force to quell the riots:

> ... the Town, redeemed,
>   Give thanks devout; nor, being thankful, heeds
>   The grimy slur on the Republic's faith implied,
>   Which holds that Man is naturally good,
>   And – more – is Nature's Roman, never to be scourged.[23]

As Milton Stern has pointed out, "In 'The House-Top' what is clear is a dominant distrust of men, a sense of the limitations of fallen man, and a consequent need for formal imposition of law and order."[24]

Some thirteen years later in his long poem *Clarel* (1876), Melville responded in a similar vein to the recent French revolution of 1871, when the communists took over Paris for two months (establishing the Paris Commune), and thousands of people were killed before and after government troops regained the city. In the poem, he portrays the "Reds" as even more reprehensible than the French revolutionaries of 1789:

> The Revolution, whose first mode,
>   Ere yet the maniacs overrode,
>   Despite the passion of the dream
>   Evinced no disrespect for God; ...
>   But yesterday – how did they then,

In new uprising of the Red,
The offspring of those Tuileries men?
They made a clothes-stand of the Cross
Before the church; . . .
Transcended rebel angels.[25]

In other words, the revolutionaries become like Lucifer's minions, angels who revolt against God and are cast into hell. This demonization of French revolutionaries is attributed to Ungar, the disillusioned Confederate soldier in *Clarel*, but it forms part of the overall political conservatism of the poem. As Walter E. Bezanson has pointed out, "A major political theme of *Clarel*" is "intense distrust of French revolutionary politics in the 19th century, and of radicalism generally."[26] Throughout *Clarel*, a number of Melville's characters, including Rolfe, the Dominican, Mortmain, and Ungar, heap contempt upon the "Vitriolists," "Red Caps," "Communists," and "Atheists."

As he worked on *Billy Budd*, until shortly before his death in 1891, Melville returned to the 1789 Revolution in France, surely because of contemporary social unrest.[27] He addressed this unrest obliquely, however, reasserting his sense of the cyclical nature of human events and making his indictment of radicalism transhistorical and sweeping. The "Great Mutiny," we are told, was precipitated by revolution in France, yet it resembled "what a strike in the fire-brigade would be to London threatened by general arson" (54). Melville thus links mutiny, revolution, strikes, and arson through their common destructivness. The special urgency of the situation on the *Bellipotent* arises because Billy's killing of Claggart occurs during wartime, at a time when the future of the Western world depends upon Vere's ability to maintain control of his ship. As the narrator explains, "The year 1797, the year of this narrative, belongs to a period which, as every thinker now feels, involved a crisis for Christendom not exceeded in its undetermined

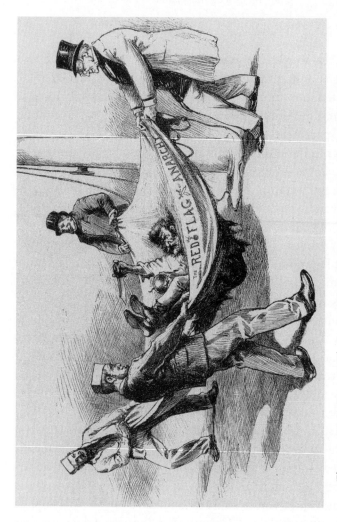

Figure 3 W. A. Rogers, *The Latest Chicago Idea: Tossing the Anarchist in His Own Blanket –
The Red Flag.*

momentousness at the time by any other era whereof there is record."[28] The "crisis" provides the justification for, and clarifies the stakes involved in, Vere's stern justice.

In the early drafts of *Billy Budd*, one can see Melville's strong antipathy toward the French Revolution of 1789, as he stresses its violence and bloodshed. In subsequent drafts, perhaps in an effort to emphasize Vere's solidity and reason, he tones down the narrative's extremism and adds weight to its conservative thrust. For example, in the first account of Vere's opposition to French thought, Melville writes that the "new-fangled" ideas from abroad so far partook "of the unsound as to border on the insane." He later revised this to read "at war with the peace of the world and the true welfare of mankind."[29] French radicalism thus becomes a momentous social danger rather than a temporary psychotic state. The red flag, associated with anarchy in contemporary America, as well as revolution in France, received attention in the contemporary press and became another image Melville altered as he worked on his text. When *Harper's Weekly* applauded Chicago election results in the spring of 1887, it used a cartoon by W. A. Rogers showing an anarchist being tossed in a ragged red flag (see Figure 1.3). Melville's first description of the transformation of the British flag by the mutineers at the Spithead and the Nore, likewise treats the red flag contemptuously, as it details how the sailors wiped out the union and the cross and thereby transmuted their flag into the enemy's "red rag of revolt and universal revolution." Melville later changed this to "red meteor of unbridled and unbounded revolt,"[30] thereby granting the red flag more consequence and power.

The British colors at the time had no cross to be wiped out, as Stanton Garner has shown,[31] yet the historical inaccuracy allows Melville to suggest symbolically the anti-Christian and atheistical dimensions of revolution, as he had done previously in *Moby-Dick* and *Clarel*, where he alluded to the French revolutions of 1848 and 1871 respectively. In *Moby-Dick*, the red flag of revolt flying on the mast-head of the *Pequod* is linked symbolically not only to Ahab's mad rebellion against God, but also to the recent "Bloody June Days" in Paris, when workers, shouting communist slogans, clashed with government troops. The tableau at the end of the novel, with its vivid conjunction of the red flag, the red arm, the hammer, the sinking ship, and the imminent descent to Hell, reflects both Melville's conservatism and contemporary attitudes toward European "Red Republicanism," which frightened Americans at mid-century.[32] Viewed in the context of Melville's earlier treatments, Captain Vere's death in *Billy Budd*, the result of a musket-ball fired from the French man-of-war, the *Atheé*, the Atheist, can be seen as Melville's last and most dramatic example of the murderous nature of French radicalism.

III

Melville's antipathy toward revolutionary action, his appreciation for law and order, flowed from a number of sources, many of them biographical. The French Revolution of 1789 was linked in his memory with the reversals of fortune of his father, his uncle Thomas, and especially himself, and it formed the basis for his latent antipathy; the French Revolution of 1848 inspired him to express this antipathy in his works, *Mardi* and *Moby-Dick*, especially; and the revolution of 1871 intensified what he already felt and believed. Violence appalled him, and he had little faith that political uprisings, even when they led to new forms of government, brought lasting benefits. One of his deepest convictions was that "'All is Vanity.' ALL," a quotation from Ecclesiastes, which he called the "fine hammered steel of woe."[33] In his view, revolutions merely resulted in one oppressor replacing another in an endless chain of oppositions. In *Mardi*, the mysterious scroll declares that "though crimson republics may rise in constellations, like fiery Aldebarans, speeding to their culminations; yet, down must they sink at last, and leave the old sultan-sun in the sky; in time, again to be deposed" (527). In "Benito Cereno," Melville uses masked images on the stern-piece — "a dark satyr in a mask, holding his foot on the prostrate neck of a writhing figure, likewise masked"[34] — to suggest that revolt, such as that on the *San Dominick*, makes victim and victimizer indistinguishable and interchangeable. In *Clarel*, Rolfe reflects on the European revolutions of 1848, writing:

> The flood weaves out — the ebb
> Weaves back; the incessant shuttle shifts
> And flies, and wears and tears the web.
> Turn, turn thee to the proof that sifts:
>
> What if the kings in Forty-Eight
> Fled like the gods? even as the gods
> Shall do, return they made; and sate
> And fortified their strong abodes.[35]

The poem thus alludes to the failures of the revolutions of 1848 and the reinstitution of new absolutist governments in almost all the countries in which revolutions occurred. In *Billy Budd*, Melville reasserts this fatalistic view of revolution, as he historicizes his narrative: "The opening proposition made by the Spirit of that Age," he writes, "involved the rectification of the Old World's hereditary wrongs. In France, to some extent, this was bloodily effected. But what then? Straightaway the Revolution regency as righter of wrongs itself became a wrongdoer, one more oppressive than the Kings. Under Napoleon it enthroned upstart kings, and initiated that prolonged agony of Continental war whose final throe was at Waterloo."[36]

Despite this fatalistic attitude toward political change, tied to his pessimistic view of mankind, Melville in his later life evidenced a Vere-like sense of duty that sustained him. As Stanton Garner has shown, the New York Custom House, where Melville worked for nineteen years until 1885, was "a genuinely malign instrument of corruption." "Out of its continual round of politics and ruthless manipulation, as well as its demand for obsequious compliance, he was forced to salvage as best he could the self-respect and dignity which were the defenses of his old age."[37] When Melville began his service, he wore a badge on the outside of his coat, and beginning early in 1878 he and the other inspectors wore Navy-like uniforms modeled on those of the Revenue Cutter Service.[38] When Vere tells his drum-head court that the buttons on their uniforms attest that their allegiance is to the King, not to Nature, he expresses a sense of duty that Melville evidenced in his own service to the state. In 1873 his brother-in-law John C. Hoadley thus described Melville's conduct: "surrounded by low venality, he puts it all quietly aside, – quietly declining offers of money for special services, – quietly returning money which has been thrust into his pockets behind his back, avoiding offence alike to the corrupting merchants and their clerks and runners, who think that all men can be bought, and to the corrupt swarms who shamelessly seek their price."[39] On points of honor, Melville was obstinate, and despite his explorations of cultural relativism and epistomolgical uncertainty, much of his thought rested upon a foundation of ethical certainty. At the heart of Melville's great work, *Moby-Dick,* lies an obsession with justice, and Ahab's quarrel with the god or gods who allow the faithful and innocent to suffer can be read as an insistence that life should resemble a boxing match where strict rules apply. *Billy Budd* marks Melville's final exploration of this topic and offers the insight that justice itself can cause the faithful and innocent to suffer. It should be added, though, that Billy's violent streak and his failure to report a mutiny in the making call into question his putative innocence.

In his interactions with members of his family, especially his sons, Melville displayed a firmness much like Vere's, which set him apart. Vere, we are told, "though a conscientious disciplinarian, . . . was no lover of authority for mere authority's sake" (104), and one suspects Melville thought of himself in the same way. As Merton Sealts has pointed out, Melville "was a strict disciplinarian, given to moodiness and irascibility that some of his relatives by marriage came to interpret as outright insanity."[40] In his dealings with his own children, he seems to have been inflexible, and circumstantial evidence suggests that the suicide of his son Malcolm in 1867 may have been precipitated by Melville's harsh discipline. Hennig Cohen and Donald Yannella have posited that "For Malcolm, caught between a kindly though inept mother and a domineering father and trapped within an atmosphere of matrimonial tension, there was no substitute for pistol and ball."[41] Though one hesitates to accept this assertion, knowledge of Melville's troubled relations with Malcolm accentuates the poignancy of the last embrace between Billy and Vere, which remains veiled from our eyes. Melville writes of the scene, "two of great Nature's nobler order embrace. There is privacy at the time, inviolable to the survivor; and holy oblivion, the sequel to each diviner magnanimity, providentially covers all at last" (115). If Melville's treatment of Vere draws upon the author's own experiences, then Billy's forgiveness of Vere should perhaps be read as a father's wishful fantasy about hearing his dead son speak.

The fact that Vere and Billy are portrayed as exceptional men gives us additional reason to view them in the context of Melville's life and career. Vere's rigidity as well as Billy's goodness are Christlike within Melville's sociopolitical system of values. Sometime after receiving a copy of *New Testament & Psalms* as a gift in 1846, Melville copied and underscored the following description of Christ into the book:

> In Life he appears as a true Philosopher – as a wise man in the highest sense. He stands *firm to his point*; he *goes on his way inflexibly*; and while he exalts the lower to himself, while he makes the ignorant, the poor, the sick, partakers of his wisdom, of his riches, of his strength, he, on the other hand, in no wise conceals his divine origin; he dares to equal himself with God; nay to declare that he himself is God.
>
> In this manner is he wont from youth upwards to *astonish his familiar friends*; of these he gains a part to his own cause; irritates the rest against him; and shows to all men, who are aiming at a certain elevation in doctrine and life, *what they have to look for from the world*.[42]

This interpretation of the character and life of Christ not only captures Melville's sense of his own "inflexibility," but also illuminates his admiration for Vere's firmness. Near the end of his life, as he was revising *Billy Budd*, Melville marked several book passages that reveal his continued fascination with the superior individual. In Balzac's *Fame and Sorrow* he scored a passage describing "the horrible strife, the incessant warfare which mediocrity wages against superior men," and in Schopenhauer's *Studies in Pessimism*, he scored, "... if he is a man of genius, he will occasionally feel like some noble prisoner of state, condemned to work in the galleys with common criminals; and he will follow his example and try to isolate himself."[43] These passages help us understand Melville's conception of himself, of Vere, and perhaps even of Billy.

Of all the qualities linking Vere and Billy to one another, the noble blood flowing in their veins is the most telling, and it sets them apart from the turbulent masses. Despite his democracy,

Melville believed that "blood will tell," and we should see
no irony in his insistence that "noble descent was as evident
in [Billy] as in a blood horse" (52). Melville had made the
same point about King Mehevi in *Typee* (1846), Jack Chase
in *White-Jacket*, and Queequeg in *Moby-Dick*. Like his own
father and mother, Melville prided himself on his ancestry,
and he named his son Malcolm after Scottish nobility. In 1850,
Melville told Sophia Hawthorne and she reported to her sis-
ter, that he was "of Scotch descent – of noble lineage – of the
Lords of Melville & Leven, & Malcolm is a family name."[44]
Like Jack Chase, to whom *Billy Budd* is dedicated, Billy is
a "by-blow," a noble foundling, whose "small and shapely"
ear, "the arch of the foot, the curve in mouth and nostril,"
expression, attitude, and movement all "strangely indicated a
lineage in direct contradiction to his lot" (51). As many readers
have noticed, he could thus be Vere's actual, as well as surrogate, son.

While Melville privileged blood and respected the eleva-
tion it conferred, he had no blind faith in authority. *Billy Budd*
argues on behalf of law, order, social stability, and family solidarity, but our reading is complicated by indications that here,
as in *White-Jacket*, Melville views with contempt those who
represent established order yet act to subvert it. The villain,
Claggart, after all, is master-at-arms, the chief policeman on
the ship; it is he who seeks to engage Billy in mutiny. This
feature of the book returns us to the 1880s and the labor unrest
surrounding Melville as he wrote. Although the police were
applauded in the press for protecting citizens and preserving
order during turbulent times, the public had gradually become
aware that some law enforcement officers actively engaged
in infiltrating labor organizations and inciting the riots that
brought the law to bear upon striking workers. Having gained
its reputation in the suppression of the Molly Maguires during

the 1870s, the Pinkerton Agency advertised its espionage services by claiming that "corporations and individuals desirous
of ascertaining the feeling of their employees and whether
they are likely to engage in strikes or are joining any secret
labor organization with a view of compelling terms from corporations or employers, can obtain . . . a detective suitable to
associate with their employees."[45] Pinkerton agents, however,
often acted, like Claggart, as *agents provocateurs*, who created
trouble rather than prevented it. As John McBride, president
of the United Mine Workers, pointed out, the Pinkertons
"had an interest in keeping up and creating troubles which
gave employers opportunity to demand protection from the
state militia at the expense of the state."[46] In some cities, the
police operated in a similar fashion. In an interview given
in May 1889 Chicago Chief of Police Frederick Ebersold admitted that in the wake of the Haymarket bombing, the police
had organized anarchist societies, planted bombs and weapons
at their headquarters, and then raided these. One anarchist
and *agent provocateur* may even have thrown the Haymarket
bomb.[47]

   Though Claggart and Vere both represent the forces of
law and order on the *Bellipotent*, the former forsakes his du-
ties while the latter does not, and Melville suggests that the
foreign element in Claggart's blood is tied to his despica-
ble behavior. Unlike Billy and Vere, he is not English by
birth. He speaks with "a bit of an accent" (65) and seems
vaguely French. Rumor has it that he was a "*chevalier*" previously involved in "some mysterious swindle" (65). Melville's
lifelong association of France with revolutionary violence
may thus inform his characterization of Claggart as may
American prejudice against foreigners as a whole. As Susan
Mizruchi has pointed out, "Claggart's story resembles a type
of fantasy about immigration that captivated Americans in

the 1880s, especially those of Vere's class: . . . the arrival of the alien serpent introduces social chaos."[48] Like Satan, Claggart reveals his demonic "otherness" through his subversive activities.

As for the "people" on the *Bellipotent*, Melville portrays them, as he does the common sailors in his other works, as easily manipulated both by the Veres and Claggarts of the world. More ignorant than depraved, they lack the acuity to do more than respond to the material facts of their existence. "Yes, as a class, sailors are in character a juvenile race," the narrator declares. "Even their deviations are marked by juvenility" (87). What then is the appropriate response to these undeveloped men when they become lawless and violent? Superior force seems to be one answer couched in the story of Billy's encounter with Red Whiskers on *The Rights of Man*. After the fellow "insultingly gave him a dig under the ribs," Billy "gave the burly fool a terrible drubbing" (47). As a result, this fiery fellow ends up loving Billy. Vere, too, evokes Billy's love, or at least his blessing, when he uses force against him. "Baby" Budd's crime is that he strikes – instinctually, irrationally, murderously. Vere, after "the father in him . . . was replaced by the military disciplinarian" (100), strikes back – thoughtfully, rationally, lawfully. In Melville's eyes, Vere thus demonstrates a right response to popular violence, when the times are revolutionary.

NOTES

1 Herman Melville, *Correspondence*, ed. Lynn Horth (Evanston and Chicago: Northwestern University Press and The Newberry Library, 1993), p. 191.
2 John Swinton, *Striking for Life*, New York, 1894, preface, quoted in Philip S. Foner, *History of the Labor Movement in the United States: Volume II: From the Founding of the American Federation of Labor*

to the Emergence of American Imperialism (New York: International Publishers, 1955), p. 11.

3　Alan Trachtenberg, *The Incorporation of America: Culture & Society in the Gilded Age* (New York: Hill and Wang, 1982), pp. 88–89. For studies of labor unrest during these years, see Paul Avrich, *The Haymarket Tragedy* (Princeton University Press, 1984); Henry David, *The History of the Haymarket Affair: A Study in the American Social-Revolutionary and Labor Movements* (New York: Russell & Russell, 1936); Philip S. Foner, *The Great Labor Uprising of 1877* (New York: Monad Press, 1977) and *History of the Labor Movement in the United States: Volume II*; and David Montgomery, "Strikes in Nineteenth Century America," *Social Science History* (February 1980): 81–104.

4　See, for example, the cartoon entitled "The Pirate Ship – Will the Socialists Capture the City Government?" in the *Daily Illustrated Graphic*, October 5, 1886; see also, Foner, *History of the Labor Movement*, 2: 126, and Trachtenberg, *Incorporation*, 88. It should be noted that the attitude toward workers was more sympathetic in rural and small town America; see Herbert G. Gutman, "The Worker's Search for Power: Labor in the Gilded Age," in *The Gilded Age: A Reappraisal*, ed. H. Wayne Morgan (Syracuse University Press, 1963), pp. 38–68.

5　*Harper's Weekly* 30 (March 13, 1886): 172.

6　The facts here are taken from Foner, *History*, 2:106.

7　Quoted in Foner, *History*, 2:111.

8　Foner, *History*, 2:116.

9　*Harper's Weekly* 31 (October 1, 1887): 702.

10　*New York Times*, (November 25, 1887): 4.

11　*Harper's Weekly* 31 (November 26, 1887): 849–52.

12　For an account of the pardon and reaction to it, see Avrich, *Haymarket Tragedy*, 415–27.

13　Trachtenberg, *Incorporation*, 203.

14　Robert K. Wallace, "*Billy Budd* and the Haymarket Hangings," *American Literature* 47 (1975): 108–13 argues that *Billy Budd* "reflects the author's imaginative response to the Haymarket affair" (108), and he points out parallels between Melville's novel and Haymarket developments. In his *Subversive Genealogy: The Politics and Art of Herman Melville* (New York: Knopf, 1983), Michael Rogin also observes that "Melville began *Billy Budd* in the aftermath of the Haymarket Affair. The social upheaval and corruption of the Gilded Age had made the state fragile once again. It required the modern hero, Captain Vere, to support it" (284). In "From Empire to Empire: *Billy Budd, Sailor*," in *Herman Melville: Reassessments*, ed. A. Robert Lee (Totowa, N.J.: Barnes & Noble, 1984), pp. 199–216, H. Bruce Franklin draws upon Wallace's 1975 article and sets out the case against Vere, citing as part of the immediate background of *Billy Budd* "the secret police whose machinations led to the Haymarket bombing and the railroading of the workers' leaders in the ensuing trials" (212). Susan Mizruchi in "Cataloging the Creatures of the Deep: 'Billy Budd, Sailor' and the Rise of Sociology," *Boundary 2* 17 (1990): 272–304, also takes issue with Rogin's positive view of Vere, though she too ties the book to contemporary social developments, especially immigration and the rise of sociology; for her "the story testifies to Melville's deep engagement with the growing diversity of American society and the variety of responses to it" (276, n. 7).

15 Judge Joseph E. Gary, who presided over the Haymarket trial, displayed extraordinary bias. He refused to disqualify prospective jurors who admitted their prejudice against the defendants; he even allowed the relative of one of the slain policemen to serve on the jury; he made repeated remarks during the trial revealing his contempt and hostility towards the accused; he ruled in favor of the prosecution on every contested point; and he allowed the prosecution to heap abuse upon the defendants during the closing arguments; see Avrich, *Haymarket Tragedy*, 262–66.

Cindy Weinstein has examined the parallels between Gary's judicial conduct and Vere's, arguing that both manipulated the law to insure a guilty verdict: "The Performative Body in *Billy Budd*," a paper presented at the American Studies Association Meeting in Boston, November 1993.

16 Milton R. Stern, "Introduction" to Herman Melville, *Billy Budd* ed. Milton R. Stern (Indianapolis: Bobbs-Merrill, 1975), p. 10, n. 12.

17 *Billy Budd, Sailor (An Inside Narrative)*, ed. Harrison Hayford and Merton M. Sealts, Jr. (University of Chicago Press, 1962), pp. 112–13. Hereafter cited parenthetically in the text.

18 See my "Kings and Commoners in *Moby-Dick*," *Studies in the Novel*, 12 (Summer 1980): 101–13.

19 Herman Melville, *Moby-Dick*, ed. Harrison Hayford, Hershel Parker, and G. Thomas Tanselle (Evanston and Chicago: Northwestern University Press and The Newberry Library, 1988), p. 466.

20 See my *European Revolutions and the American Literary Renaissance* (New Haven: Yale University Press, 1988), pp. 97–124.

   Melville's response to the Astor Place Riots in May 1849 was consistent with his response to revolutions abroad. Along with forty-seven prominent citizens of New York City, he signed a letter of support for the British actor William Charles Macready, whose appearance at the Astor Place Opera House was protested by members of New York's laboring classes, supporters of Macready's arch rival, the American actor Edwin Forrest. On the evening of May 10, a mob of 10 to 20,000 gathered to disrupt Macready's performance in *Macbeth*; when they threw rocks and invaded the theater, the militia opened fire, and some 31 persons were killed and 150 wounded. The letter Melville signed assured Macready "that the good sense and respect for order prevailing in this community will sustain you on the subsequent nights of your performance" (quoted in Richard Moody, *The Astor Place Riot* (Bloomington: Indiana University Press, 1958), p. 116).

21 *Mardi: And a Voyage Thither*, ed. Harrison Hayford, Hershel Parker, and G. Thomas Tanselle (Evanston and Chicago: Northwestern University Press and The Newberry Library, 1970), p. 499. Hereafter cited parenthetically in the text.

22 Herman Melville, *Collected Poems of Herman Melville*, ed. Howard P. Vincent (Chicago: Hendricks House, 1947), p. 15. Gail Coffer has astutely discussed the combining of the actual and the ideal in Melville's *Battle Pieces*; see her "Form as Resolution: Classical Elements in Melville's *Battle Pieces*," in *American Poetry: Between Tradition and Modernism, 1865–1914*, ed. Roland Hagenbüchle (n.p. Verlag Friedrich Pustet Regensburg, 1984), pp. 105–21.

23 Melville, *Collected Poems*, 57.

24 Stern, "Introduction," in Herman Melville, *Billy Budd*, ed. Milton R. Stern (New York: Bobbs-Merrill, 1975), p. xxvii. Stern provides the fullest account to date of the conservatism of *Billy Budd*, which

he traces to the politics of Melville's poetry, especially the Civil War poems.

25 Herman Melville, *Clarel*, ed. Walter E. Bezanson (New York: Hendricks House, 1960), pp. 478–79.

26 Bezanson, "Explanatory Notes," in *Clarel*, 587.

27 Brook Thomas has also noted that plans for celebrating the centenary of the first French Revolution turned American attention to the subject; see his *Cross-examinations of Law and Literature: Cooper, Hawthorne, Stowe, and Melville* (Cambridge University Press, 1987), p. 239.

28 Melville, *Billy Budd*, ed. Stern, 97–98. This quotation does not appear in the Hayford and Sealts edition of *Billy Budd*, but as Stern has argued, there is no absolute proof Melville discarded the manuscript leaves on which it appears and thus they should be included rather than excluded in editions of the work.

29 *Billy Budd: The Genetic Text*, ed. Harrison Hayford and Merton M. Sealts, Jr. (University of Chicago Press, 1962), p. 313.

30 Ibid., 300.

31 Stanton Garner, "Fraud as Fact in Herman Melville's *Billy Budd*," *San Jose Studies* 4 (1978): 85–105.

32 Reynolds, *European Revolutions*, 122.

33 Melville, *Moby-Dick*, 424.

34 Herman Melville, *The Piazza Tales, and Other Prose Pieces, 1839–1860*, ed. Harrison Hayford, Alma A. MacDougall, and G. Thomas Tanselle (Evanston and Chicago: Northwestern University Press and The Newberry Library, 1987), p. 49.

35 Melville, *Clarel*, 157.

36 Melville, *Billy Budd*, ed. Stern, 98.

37 Stanton Garner, "Melville in the Custom House, 1881–1882: A Rustic Beauty Among the Highborn Dames of Court," *Melville Society Extracts* (1978) 35: 14.

38 Ibid., 9.

39 Jay Leyda, *The Melville Log: A Documentary Life of Herman Melville, 1819–1891*, 2 vols. (1951; rpt. with additional material, New York: Gordian Press, 1969) 2: 731.

40 Merton M. Sealts, "Innocence and Infamy: *Billy Budd, Sailor*," in *A Companion to Melville Studies*, ed. John Bryant (New York: Greenwood Press, 1986), p. 416.

41 *Herman Melville's Malcolm Letter: "Man's Final Lore"* (New York: Fordham University Press and The New York Public Library, 1992), pp. 56–60. Cohen and Yannella show that members of the Melville-Gansevoort family, including Melville himself, used authoritarian methods of childrearing to produce dutiful children and to maintain family strength and solidarity. Edwin S. Shneidman, a clinical psychologist, has argued "that Herman Melville himself had been a psychologically 'battered child' and, in a way typical for battered children, psychologically battered his own children when it came to be his turn to be a parent"; see "Some Psychological Reflections on the Death of Malcolm Melville," *Suicide and Life-Threatening Behavior*, 6 (1976): 231–42.

42 Eleanor Metcalf, *Herman Melville: Cycle and Epicycle* (Cambridge, Mass.: Harvard University Press, 1953), p. 38.

43 Leyda, *Log*, 2: 830, 832.

44 Quoted in Leyda, *Log*, 2: 296.

45 Quoted in M. B. Schnapper, *American Labor: A Pictorial Social History* (Washington, D. C.: Public Affairs Press, 1972), p. 113.

46 Quoted in Ibid., 111.

47 See Foner, *History*, 2: 107–11.

48 Mizruchi, "Cataloging," 297.

Religion, myth, and meaning in the art of Billy Budd, Sailor

Gail Coffler

Though I wrote the Gospels in this century, I should die
in the gutter –[1]

I

Melville's classic tale of the Handsome Sailor yields numerous
interpretations. For me, *Billy Budd* is less a sea story than an
allegorical fable about the relationship of truth to art. On the
epistemological level, the tale illustrates how truth shifts during the creative process; here Melville uses elements of myth
to question the Bible's truth. On an aesthetic level, *Billy Budd*
reveals Melville's theory of art: the conflict between Billy and
Claggart dramatizes the essential dialectic between the forces
of light and dark, Hellenism and Hebraism. Finally, Vere as
executor performs the crucial act necessary to transform Billy
into a mythic hero.

The dialogical argument that had sustained Melville's long
poem *Clarel* (1876), whether Christianity was "true" or not,
was an issue in *Moby-Dick* (1851), *The Confidence-Man* (1857),
and all his major works as a corollary to the larger epistemological problem: whether objective truth exists and if humans
can ever know anything with certitude. As in "Benito Cereno,"
Billy Budd, Sailor first presents the two central characters
from a third person's "inside" point of view, then reverses our

perspective with an "historical" footnote. Billy is presented
as the archetypal hero while Claggart is the corrupt villain.
Though Billy clearly violated military law, we are persuaded of
the "exceptional" nature of the case: Billy was defending himself against a lie, and his killing of Claggart was unintentional.
For readers whose ethics are influenced by Judaeo-Christian
teachings, Graeco-Roman law and philosophy, and a long
history of romantic individualism, Billy is morally innocent
and the navy report at the end is completely false. We should
remember, however, that our judgment has been predeter-
mined by the narrative's subjective viewpoint which, like its
allusions to religion and myth, is slanted entirely in the hero's
favor.

At one point in the narrative, we are warned: "In the jug-
glery of circumstances . . . innocence and guilt personified in
Claggart and Budd in effect changed places"[2]: originally, then,
Claggart was innocent and Budd guilty. And this is exactly the
case. The Hayford and Sealts Genetic Text reveals the original
Billy Budd and how he evolved over more than five years. In
late 1885, Melville first wrote the ballad "Billy in the Darbies,"
a sailor's reverie on the eve of his execution for a crime he
likely committed.[3] Later, Melville expanded the work into a
short tale. By 1888, when he again enlarged the story, Billy
had changed.

From the "Captain of a gun crew," and a much older man,
Billy became a young foretopman. Moreover, Billy-in-the-
Darbies originally confessed: "My little game is up."[4] But
by the time Melville died in 1891, Billy had become one of
Nature's noblemen: "welkin-eyed Billy Budd – or Baby Budd,
as . . . he at last came to be called" (44).

In the reforming process, as Melville idealized Billy, innocence and guilt indeed "changed places": the original (guilty)
Billy was reduced to a name in the navy report near the end

on a doorstep but he is of "noble" birth; and Billy's lack
of movement at death is "phenomenal."

Billy Budd, Sailor (An Inside Narrative) is the Handsome
Sailor myth in full bud. The tale is told decades later by an unknown narrator, who calls Billy a "peacemaker" and "moral
phenomenon." Billy's mysterious birth and "phenomenal"
death, his fatal flaw and "extraordinary" nature, Vere's revelation of him as "an angel of God," all combine in an image
of Billy that transcends the "human record" (131). However,
this surface portrait of a god-like figure contains ambiguities
that undermine the story's "truth."[7]

II

From its opening, the narrative hints of discrepancies between
natural truth and the "truth" perpetuated in religion and myth.
Melville establishes the Handsome Sailor ideal by connecting
Billy to classical and biblical heroes, each known for "strength
and beauty" (44). In the light of these mythological peers,
Billy's image is increasingly enhanced. However, the narration omits the negative spots in each hero's legend, giving
a superficial and blandly positive impression. The result is a
whitewash.

For example, when the narrator recalls an "intensely black"
sailor on the Liverpool docks, "a native African of the unadul-
terate blood of Ham," he says that all wayfarers paid the
African a "spontaneous tribute . . . the tribute of a pause and
stare, and less frequently an exclamation" (43–44). But what
manner of stare? What words of exclamation? The description idealizes the situation of Africans at that time. One irony
is that the real "tribute" paid to the "strength and beauty"
of Africans was enslavement. Another irony is that white

of the tale, and the younger (innocent) Billy emerg
primary position. Thus the ideal Billy became what
now see as the "real" Billy. "But aren't it all sham?" The i
ical question expressed in the ballad has new implications
one understands Billy's origins. One critic has suggested
narrator's idealized portrait of Billy . . . is literally 'too
to be true.'"[5]

Billy Budd resembles conventional myth, which idealize
it progresses from the seminal event. It typically begins w
the death of a popular hero who has violated an import;
societal code. Though his punishment is said to be deserve
his admirers see him as a savior and victim. Because he is sacre
to one faction and anathema to another, the mythic hero is bot
"blessed" and "cursed." As the myth evolves, the hero is freec
from blame: he "did indeed do what he is accused of, but *he
did not do it intentionally*"; or he is "a perfectly good hero"
who attacked "a perfectly bad monster." Related to this is
the tragic flaw – the Greek notion of *hamartia*: the hero has
"a very minor fault, a single chink in a homogeneous mass
of irreproachable virtue."[6] Finally, a mystery surrounds the
hero's birth or a miracle occurs at his death. These traits in
Billy Budd are unmistakable signs of the tale's mythopoetic
quality:

1) *gradual idealization:* Billy evolves from rude gunner and
   mutineer to Baby Budd and Handsome Sailor;
2) *"poetic minimization" of fault:* Billy did not mean to kill;
   and Billy's act was justified because Claggart lied;
3) *dualism:* inside narrative = good Billy killed evil Claggart;
   the navy's version = good Claggart was killed by evil Billy;
4) *the tragic flaw:* Billy's stutter made him strike Claggart;
5) *mysterious birth and/or miracle at death:* asked about his
   parentage, Billy replies, "God knows . . . "; he was found

Christians called Africans the "sons of Ham" in order to justify
slavery. As Melville well knew, many church-goers believed
Noah's "curse upon Ham" meant that God ordained blacks
(the supposed descendants of Ham's son, Canaan) to serve
whites.[8]

It is the *missing connection* – exactly how "Ham" is related
to Billy – that provides the essential keys to interpretation: 1)
irony: the ebony "son of Ham" is admired, but the situation
is not as handsome as its surface; 2) credibility: the narration omits significant details; 3) foreshadowing: like a "son of
Ham," Billy will be enslaved and finally lynched.

Similarly, the comparison of Billy to "young Alexander
curbing the fiery Bucephalus" (44) glosses over the interest-
ing complexities of the Greek warrior's life: the battles and
conquests, his marriages and male lovers, his mysterious death
and deification. The apocryphal taming of Bucephalus, signi-
fying the prince's "future unconquerable spirit,"[9] is in fact
the only uncontroversial part of Alexander's legend.

As to the virtue of the Handsome Sailor, the narrator says,
"The moral nature was seldom out of keeping with the physical make" (44), referring to the Greek idea that exterior beauty
reflects interior goodness. However, the statement's ambiguity allows room for interpretation according to one's cultural
standards; for example, homosexual love was completely ac-
ceptable among ancient Greeks but taboo among Hebrews.
Following the allusion to Alexander, the narrator seems pur-
posely equivocal in describing the "nature" of the handsome
sailor: "Such a cynosure, *at least in aspect*, and *something* such
too in nature, though *with important variations* made apparent
as the story proceeds was . . . Baby Budd" (44; my emphasis).

Billy is also the young Achilles being tutored by the centaur
Chiron (71). By alluding to the Greek hero, the tale establishes
Billy's athleticism and courage. Yet readers who remember

Achilles' vulnerable heel will sense that Billy's stutter will lead to his death. They should also recall Achilles' "wrath" over the death of Patroclus and his violent revenge upon Hector. While presenting a superficial image of Billy/Achilles as young and innocent, the narrative silently hints that, like his Greek prototype, the sailor has a "tragic flaw" and a deadly "wrath."

Melville's narrator omits all violence connected with these heroes, even Hercules. Every child in Melville's time knew the legend of the strongman who acted before thinking. As a baby he strangled two snakes in his crib. But years later, while temporarily "insane," he "unintentionally" killed his two children.[10] For this, he was assigned twelve labors (involving more killing) after which he was "translated to the gods."[11] Despite the strongman's violent temper, Melville's description almost makes one think Hercules was a relaxed and "good-natured" fellow: "[Billy] showed in face that humane look of *reposeful good nature* which the Greek sculptor in some instances gave to his heroic strong man, Hercules. But this again was subtly modifed by another and pervasive quality" (51; my emphasis). In his circuitous style, the narrator actually says that "the Greek sculptor in some instances *gave* to . . . Hercules" the "humane look of reposeful good nature"; in other words, an artist *endowed* him with this trait, and in Billy even this was "subtly modified" by a different and "pervasive quality." This important distinction between what existed in nature and what the sculptor "gave" his subject is what separates actuality from art. Paradoxically, great art or "true Art" is not completely "true" to nature.

The allusion to Hercules underscores Billy's brawn rather than brain and also foreshadows heroic feats. But some readers will recognize Melville's ambiguity and irony, for if Hercules had a "good nature," he also had a violent one and used

his strength to commit both good and evil deeds. Ironically, Hercules is killed by the poisoned blood of the Hydra he had once slain, and Billy's death results from killing the "snake" Claggart. Carried to Olympus, Hercules was given "divine honors" among the gods. Billy ironically "ascends" by hanging, but at last gains immortality through Melville's "inside narrative," which ranks him with gods and heroes.

The narrative links Billy with a dozen heroes, but omits facets of their legends that might detract from a positive impression on the reader even though all of the figures were involved in violent and controversial acts. In interpreting Melville's iconography, the reader must supply the missing links. For example, the narrator implies that Billy is as handsome as Apollo, son of Jove. As Billy boards Vere's ship, the lieutenant says, "Here he comes; and, by Jove, lugging along his chest — Apollo with his portmanteau!" (48). Billy resembles Apollo: god of sunlight, god of music, and god of the Delphi oracle.[12] However, in his role as "the archer god," Apollo killed not only the python but also all men; Apollo's "portmanteau" thus holds deadly arrows.[13] The *Apollo Belvedere*, the Hellenistic statue that in Melville's time was the world's most celebrated work of art, portrays the god as the sublime archer. He stands with one arm forward, holding the (now-missing) bow, the other arm (now missing) drawn back to shoot the (now-missing) arrow. To naive viewers, the beautiful god appears benign because his arm and death instruments are no longer visible, but art-literate viewers know he is the archer of death. Melville, having seen the statue in Rome, said the Apollo was "divine": "How well in the Apollo is expressed the idea of the perfect man. Who could better it? Can art, not life, make the ideal?"[14]

In another instance, the narrator quotes a "good-natured" poet who lived "near two thousand years ago": "Honest and

poor, faithful in word and thought,/What hath thee, Fabian,
to the city brought?" (53). The lines are from Martial, the
Roman satirist of Nero's time.[15] Though superficially "good-
natured," this epigram is stingingly ironic. Fabius Pictor
was the first Roman to write his country's history. Since
he was a member of the rich and illustrious Fabian family,
he certainly was not "poor"; thus, Martial implies, neither
was he "honest" or "faithful in word and thought." Anthon's
Classical Dictionary calls Fabius Pictor a "wretchedly qualified" historian whose account of Rome is totally false, filled
with fables and inaccuracies: "from this tainted source, have
flowed all the stories concerning Mars, the Vestal, the Wolf,
Romulus and Remus."[16] Martial's verse ironically addresses
the issue of "truthful" reporting in a supposedly historical
account, though Martial's own stance on the matter is
ambiguous.

The narrative alludes to Fabian, and by extension Billy,
as "the good rustic out of his latitude in the Rome of the
Caesars" (53) but Fabian was not literally a "rustic." It
was the Fabian book of "rustic" folklore that was out of its
"latitude" among Romans who wanted a "true" history of
Rome, one that was (politically) correct. Melville, whose
"truths" had likewise been attacked, might have sympathized
with the ancient writer who preserved myths that outlived the
fame of critics and Caesars. If one kind of "truth" has a place
in "history," another has its place in "art."

Exemplifying *Billy Budd*'s density and complexity, this
passage satirizes 1) naive readers who fail to recognize irony
in either Martial or Melville; 2) provincialists who confuse
myth and history now, as their counterparts had "two thousand years ago in Rome" (an oblique reference to Christianity,
which also blends myth and history); 3) period critics such
as Charles Anthon who regarded fables as a "completely

false" and "tainted history" instead of understanding them as myth; 4) and narrow-minded audiences in general who fail to see that "truth" is not incompatible with "fiction" or "art" or "myth"; in the hands of a skilled and thoughtful artist, they can all be one.

III

Until Billy Budd is taken on Vere's ship, he is an "upright barbarian" who lives frankly "in accordance with natural law" (52); but after he boards the *Bellipotent*, the story's *ethos* changes. "[T]ransmitted from a period prior to Cain's city and citified man," Billy had not yet been offered "the questionable apple of knowledge" (52–53). Just before he meets Claggart, Billy is described as "Adam . . . ere the urbane Serpent wriggled himself into his company" (52).

The Judaeo-Christian concept of sin enters the tale with John Claggart who brings into the story the Old Testament moral vision of human sin, an idea foreign to the ancient Greeks and Romans. The concept of sin as "a positive, active entity hostile to man" is firmly Hebraistic, stated Matthew Arnold, whose essays and poems served Melville as a mentor, especially during the 1860s and 1870s, the years when he was writing the long poem *Clarel* in an effort to resolve his own spiritual crisis.[17] Arnold's essay "Hebraism and Hellenism" in *Culture and Anarchy* (Sealts no. 16) proposed that these two cultures, which unite in Christianity, are the basis of western civilization; the idea became accepted doctrine, reaching a popular audience near the turn of the century through the novel *Robert Elsmere* (1888), by Mrs. Humphrey Ward, Arnold's niece.[18]

In *Clarel: A Poem and Pilgrimage to the Holy Land*, Melville's intense interest in the Hellenism/Hebraism debate

is characterized by Rolfe, whom Bezanson describes as a
"not unreasonable idealization" of Melville himself.[19] Rolfe
is sailor and philosopher, "seeker and skeptic combined":
"Exponent of the two great heritages of Western civilization,
the Hellenic and Hebraic worlds of value, [Rolfe] is especially
fascinated by analogies and distinctions between them."[20]
The debates between Rolfe and the other characters make
Clarel a remarkable study of comparative religion, one that
demonstrates Melville's encompassing grasp of the streams
that converged in Christianity.

While in *Clarel* the Hellenism/Hebraism issue is discussed
by the characters, in *Billy Budd* the Hebraism/Hellenism dialectic is symbolically represented in the characters and their
action. The Handsome Sailor's dominant traits – masculine
"comeliness and power" and a "moral nature . . . seldom out
of keeping" (44) – reflect the Greek view of external beauty
as a visible sign of inner beauty or goodness. But Claggart
is moved against Billy precisely because of "his significant
personal beauty" and his exceptional moral "innocence"
(77–78). Claggart possesses what Arnold describes as the
Hebraic moral conscience: awakened to a sense of sin and
disposed to religious faith, it is suspicious of beauty and pleasure and committed instead to a single-minded conception
of what is true and righteous. Whereas Hellenism gives us
hope and comfort by keeping difficulties "out of view," as
Arnold explains, Hebraism is "severely preoccupied" with
one thing: "This something is *sin*, and the space which sin
fills in Hebraism, as compared with Hellenism, is indeed
prodigious."[21] That is to say, many acts viewed by Hellenists
as innocent would be regarded by Hebraists or strict Calvinists
as sinful.

Claggart's envy of Billy was "no vulgar form of the passion," we are told, *nor* was it the "apprehensive jealousy" Saul
felt toward "the comely young David" (77–78).[22] Rather, he

had a "cynic disdain" of Billy's innocence, though "in an aesthetic way he saw the charm of it": "If *askance he eyed the good looks, cheery health, and frank enjoyment of young life* in Billy Budd, it was because these went along with a nature that, as Claggart magnetically felt, had in its simplicity never willed malice or experienced the reactionary bite of that serpent" (78; my emphasis). Suspicious of Billy's "free-and-easy temper" (78), his obliviousness to sin and evil, Claggart exhibits the "watchful jealousy" that to Arnold is the defining trait of radical Hebraism and that he identified with Puritanism and its descendants. These literal-minded dogmatists misinterpret Paul's injunction to a "godly jealousy," says Arnold in *Literature and Dogma* (Sealts no. 18); in truth, "Their 'spirit of watchful jealousy' is wholly destructive and exclusive of the spirit of Christianity."[23]

As the "chief of police charged . . . with the duty of preserving order" (64), Claggart is the operative moral guardian of the *Bellipotent* which Melville likens to a "Christian capital of our time" with Billy wandering dazed in it (53). John Claggart's initial's are J.C. – his name recalls John Calvin – and he sniffs out vice among the seamen like an overzealous Calvinist. He is compared with the Reverend Titus Oates, the fanatical Protestant who constructed the lie against the Catholic Church – "the fraud of the alleged Popish Plot" for which three innocent men were hanged.[24] The Oates reference links Claggart to the "pharisaical" church constables in *Omoo* (1847), "sent out with rattans" as "whippers-in" of the reluctant natives.[25] "These worthies constitute a *religious police* . . . going all over the island, and spying out the wickedness. . . . To be reported by one of these officials as a . . . *bad person or disbeliever in Christianity*, is as much dreaded as the forefinger of Titus Oates was, leveled at an alleged papist."[26]

Claggart is associated with radical Protestantism, but also with religious fanaticism of other breeds: "The Pharisee is the Guy Fawkes prowling in the hid chambers underlying some natures like Claggart's" (80).[27] Describing his "clandestine persecution of Billy," Melville writes, "Claggart's conscience . . . justified animosity into a sort of retributive *righteousness*" (80). According to Arnold, "The word 'righteousness,' is the *master-word* of the Old Testament" and "conduct, or 'righteousness,' . . . is in a special manner the object of Bible religion." But the true spirit of Christian righteousness is misunderstood by the narrow, single-minded dogmatists with their rigid theology and its "insane licence."[28]

Like a Puritan witch-hunter, Claggart ferrets out offenses, making "ogres of trifles" (80). His "mantle of respectability" (75) and "uncommon prudence" (80) make him practically unassailable as an officer on the King's ship, where even "the promiscuous lame ducks of morality" are "as much in sanctuary as the transgressor of the Middle Ages harboring himself under the shadow of the altar," says the narrator, whose double meaning hints of sinners within the church, protected by the priesthood (65–66).

Though outwardly respectable with a "discreet bearing," Claggart is "the direct reverse of a saint" (74), which is to say, a terrible sinner. The worst sin is Pride, and Claggart's nature has the "phenomenal pride in it that excludes vices or small sins" while it looks for sin and weakness in others (76). Claggart's nature could be explained if the "lexicon . . . based on Holy Writ" were still "popular," says the narrator, turning to an "authority not liable to the charge of being tinctured with the biblical element," to a definition in the "authentic" translation of Plato:[29] "'Natural Depravity: a depravity according to nature,' a definition which, though savoring of Calvinism, by no means involves Calvin's dogma as to total mankind . . . its intent makes it applicable but to individuals. Not many are the examples of this depravity which the gallows and jails supply" (75).

In other words, this definition "attributed" to Plato applies only to exceptional, animal-like persons, whereas Calvin's dogma holds that all humans are inherently sinful. Claggart's nature is "exceptional" but has none of the "brute" in it; it "partakes nothing of the sordid or sensual," nor is it the sort found in jails, for it is "dominated by intellectuality" (75–76). Seemingly rational, he is secretly and insanely vindictive. However, his evil is not learned but "born with him and innate; in short 'a depravity according to nature'" (76): "Dark sayings are these, some will say. But why? Is it because they somewhat savor of Holy Writ in its phrase 'mystery of iniquity'? If they do, such savor was far enough from being intended, for little will it commend these pages to many a reader today" (76). To a post-Darwin audience, "the biblical element" may be tiresome; nevertheless, these "dark sayings," these views of Claggart's nature, *do* savor of Calvinism, of Holy Writ, and of Paul's "mystery of iniquity."[30]

Claggart signifies the dark force that began to occupy Melville in the *Moby-Dick* years, when he recognized its power in Shakespeare and Hawthorne.[31] In his essay "Hawthorne and His Mosses" (1850), Melville penetrated beyond the "sunlight side" of Hawthorne to his "dark half . . . shrouded in a blackness, ten times black." Analyzing what arrested him in Hawthorne's fiction, Melville wrote,

Whether there really lurks in [Hawthorne] . . . a touch of Puritanic gloom, – this, I cannot altogether tell. Certain it is, however, that this great power of blackness in him derives its force from its appeals to that *Calvinistic sense of Innate Depravity and Original Sin*, from whose visitations, in some shape or other, no deeply thinking mind is always and wholly free.[32]

Calvin's doctrines were fundamental tenets to the young Herman, who was reared in his mother's conservative Dutch Reformed Church instead of his father's liberal Unitarianism. However, Melville's own children were brought up in his wife's Unitarian Church, which he joined later, around the time he began *Billy Budd*.[33] But even though Melville repudiated Calvinism, its strong effect on him is seen in his lifelong attacks, overt and covert, on church dogma, religiosity and hypocrisy. It is evident too in his fascination with Hawthorne's themes of secret guilt, sin and heresy. The "great power of blackness" that Melville found so fascinating in Hawthorne's fiction emerged in *Moby-Dick*, where Ahab's vision of evil gives the book profundity as a counterforce to the lighter, more genial irony of many chapters. In *Moby-Dick* Melville attains equilibrium between light and dark, the comic and tragic modes – a dialectic illumined later in "Art," a poem expressing his artistic creed:

> In placid hours well-pleased we dream
> Of many a brave unbodied scheme,
> But form to lend, pulsed life create,
> What unlike things must meet and mate:
> A flame to melt – a wind to freeze;
> Sad patience – joyous energies;
> Humility – yet pride and scorn;
> *Instinct and study*; love and hate;
> Audacity – reverence. These must mate,
> And fuse with Jacob's mystic heart,
> To wrestle with the angel – Art.[34]

The phrase "instinct and study," originally written "instinct and culture,"[35] points to Melville's reading of *Culture and Anarchy* containing Arnold's "Hebraism and Hellenism." Informed by Arnold's essay, Melville's union of "unlike things" can be understood as man's tragic consciousness of sin, death, and evil (Hebraism) fused with the joyous spirit of light, life, and freedom (Hellenism). This opposition of forces later takes concrete shape in the figures of Claggart and Billy.

The union of Hellenism and Hebraism was also a major subject of the long poem *Clarel*, where Melville explored several avenues of comparative religion in a creative effort to trace the evolution of Christianity. The "mating" of Hellenism and Hebraism is demonstrated in the Hawthorne-like character of Vine,[36] whose light and dark moods are prefigured by the frieze on the Sepulcher of Kings in Jerusalem, which Clarel studies a moment before meeting Vine:

> Palm leaves, pine apples, grapes. These bloom,
> Involved in death – to puzzle us –
> As 'twere thy line, Theocritus,
> Dark Joel's text of terror threading:
> Yes, strange that Pocahontas-wedding
> Of contraries in old belief –
> Hellenic cheer, Hebraic grief.

The great tomb symbolizes death and mutability. The fruits carved on its frieze have a double allusion. They recall Joel's prophecy of disaster to Israel, drying up the vine, and killing the palm and apple tree (*Joel* 1.12). Yet these palms and fruits are tokens of Greek pastoralism; as signs of life continuing in nature, they invalidate death.[37] They still survive here but only through the sculptor's art.

The tomb with sculpted fruits is a metaphor for another work of art – the story of Christ, which is also a "Pocahontas wedding" of contrary beliefs, Hebraism and Hellenism. In Christianity, the Jewish recognition of human suffering and death unites with the Greek emphasis on life's joys in the story of Jesus, a lawbreaking Jew who suffered and died on the cross, but whose resurrection signifies mankind's hope for eternal life. By his death, Jesus paradoxically gained immortal life *through the narrative art* of the New Testament, all of which was first written in Hellenistic Greek; in the concept of "Jesus Christ," the two cultures merge.[38]

In *Clarel* Melville traced the evolution of Christianity from Hebraism and Hellenism to try to learn whether Jehovah was "a God untrue, in myth absurd / As monstrous figment blabbed of Jove." Ten years after *Clarel*, the dual forces in Melville's artistic vision are enacted by Billy and Claggart. The Hellenism/Hebraism dichotomy is apparent as Claggart watches Billy promenading with other sailors on the deck: "[Claggart's] glance would follow *the cheerful sea Hyperion* with a . . . melancholy expression, his eyes strangely infused with incipient tears. Then would Claggart look like *the man of sorrows* . . . as if Claggart could even have loved Billy but for fate and ban" (88; my emphasis). In this scene, the "Hellenic cheer, Hebraic grief " dialectic is represented by the two characters: Billy as the "cheerful" Greek sun god, and Claggart as the "man of sorrows . . . despised and rejected of men . . . and acquainted with grief," a well-known Old Testament verse said by Christians to foretell Jesus Christ (*Isa.*53:3).

The "man of sorrows" allusion connects Claggart to an important passage in *Moby-Dick*: "*The truest of all men was the Man of Sorrows*, and the truest of all books is Solomon's, and Ecclesiastes is the fine hammered steel of woe. 'All is vanity.' ALL".[39] To the extent that Claggart, like Ahab, embodies the spirit of "The Tryworks" chapter in *Moby-Dick*, Melville partly identifies with him. However, he understands that, by itself, Claggart's dark view is a destructive force that negates life's joy and, like the scorpion, recoils upon itself: " – to be nothing more than innocent! Yet in an aesthetic way he saw the charm of it, the courageous free-and-easy temper of it, and fain would have shared it, but he despaired of it" (78). In Claggart's Hebraic view, the love of beauty and of pleasure is a dangerous "mantrap" leading to the sin and suffering warned of in the Bible.

While Billy brings to mind the genial qualities of Melville's early works that charmed a popular audience, Claggart signifies the Calvinistic awareness of sin and depravity that was an essential part of Melville's vision but that he despised for its naive literal-mindedness, its pious bigotry and hypocrisy, its authoritarian policing of sin, and its infliction of guilt and shame upon those who broke its laws. In *Moby-Dick* Melville daringly played devil's advocate by attacking orthodox Protestantism through the use of irony. Like Hawthorne, he believed that extreme Calvinism was as evil as the devils it warned against; though he knew he was trespassing in hallowed territory, he thought his irony and double meanings could not be proven. Thus, he confessed to Hawthorne, "I have written *a wicked book* and feel spotless as the lamb."[40] To Duyckinck he wrote, "I wonder if *my evil art* has raised this monster," that is, whether his book *Moby-Dick* had "raised" the real-life whale that attacked the *Ann Alexander*.[41] Melville's former mentor, a devout Episcopalian, was evidently not wholly amused by the sailor's "evil art." Duyckinck's *Literary World* had nurtured Melville's career, yet its review of *Moby-Dick* (November 22, 1851), though praising the book as an "intellectual chowder," objected to Melville's "piratical running down of creeds, [which] is, we will not say dangerous [but] out of place and uncomfortable": "We do not like to see . . . the most sacred associations of life violated and defaced. . . . Nor is it fair to inveigh against priestcraft. . . . It is a curious fact that there are no more bilious people in the world . . . than some of these very people who are constantly inveighing against the religious melancholy of priestcraft."[42]

After *Moby-Dick*, Melville's iconoclasm grew ever more daring in works like *Pierre* (1852) and *The Confidence-Man*, both of which satirize Christian hypocrisy and show the folly of practicing the idea of Christian "love" or "charity" or of taking the Bible literally in many respects. In one scene aboard the *Fidèle*, the confidence-man poses as a philanthropist and chides a misanthrope for his ironic and "churlish" remarks about mankind: "Ah, now . . . irony is so unjust; never could abide irony; something Satanic about irony. God defend me from Irony, and Satire, his bosom friend."[43] Using double irony to satirize both sides of the issue, Melville hides his own position: innocence (geniality/philanthropy) and guilt (cynicism/misanthropy) are reversible in these two characters, for the philanthropist is the devil's advocate in disguise, and the misanthrope is his innocent dupe. The idea of interchangeable guilt and innocence had sustained the tension in "Benito Cereno," and Melville would use the dialectic again in *Billy Budd*.

Through the sophistry of *The Confidence-Man*, Melville suggests that the Bible is fiction: the creator of a truly "original character" is like "the founder of a new religion," he writes, implying that Paul and the "apostolic press" created an "original character" in Jesus Christ. At the novel's end, an old man sits with the Bible: "'And so you *have* good news there, sir,'" says the Cosmopolitan. "'Too good to be true,'" injects an invisible voice. That book teaches distrust, the Cosmopolitan tells the old man, pointing to this verse: "'With much communication he will tempt thee; *he will smile upon thee, and speak thee fair.* . . . When thou hearest these things, awake in thy sleep.'"[44] This passage – from the "Wisdom of Jesus, the Son of Sirach" in the *Apocrypha* – might describe Satan, or perhaps the Cosmopolitan, or, Melville devilishly hints, it might refer to the false promise of the gospels, the "good news" of Christianity. The passage is clearly a source for the character of Claggart, "'the too-fair spoken man'" in *Billy Budd* (88).

When the Cosmopolitan goes on to reject the Bible's "wisdom," his words prefigure not only Claggart but also Billy with "the dimple in his dyed cheek" (78): "'What an ugly thing this Wisdom must be! Give me the folly that dimples the cheek, say I, rather than the wisdom that curdles the blood. . . . For how can that be trustworthy that teaches distrust?'"[45] In Melville's later work, dimpled Billy portrays the folly that trusts "the too-fair spoken man," and Claggart is his counterpart: "the wisdom that curdles the blood" and that distrusts Billy's smiles and good cheer. However, in *The Confidence-Man* as in *Billy Budd*, the qualities represented by the characters are reversible. Again playing devil's advocate, the Cosmopolitan is mocking one common argument of the virtual-Christian who claims he would rather live happily in his faith and never know he was wrong than live grimly in the certitude that there is no afterlife and be dead right. But all this irony is lost on the Bible-reading man in *The Confidence-Man* who is too busy buying a lock, money-belt, and "Counterfeit-Detector."

Like the distrustful passengers on the *Fidèle*, Claggart suspects Billy is "a dangerous character" (92). He tells Vere, "You have but noted his fair cheek. A mantrap may be under the ruddy-tipped daisies" (94). To Vere at this moment, Claggart looks like "the spokesman of the envious children of Jacob [showing] the troubled patriarch the blood-dyed coat of young Joseph" (96). In the cabin scene, Vere is likened to Jacob (Israel) and Claggart to one of Jacob's sons, who betrayed their brother Joseph.[46]

Mesmerized by Claggart's "serpent" eye, representing the knowledge of sin, Billy when accused looks like a "vestal priestess in the moment of being buried alive" (99).[47] Billy's face is "a crucifixion to behold" as his fist collides with Claggart's "intellectual" forehead; then the master-at-arms lies on the floor like a "dead snake" (99). The three characters in this scene enact the final lines of Melville's poem "Art," when contrary forces "meet and mate . . . And fuse with Jacob's mystic heart, / To wrestle with the angel — Art."[48]

"It is the divine judgment on Ananias! . . . Struck dead by an angel of God! Yet the angel must hang!" (100–101). Vere's exclamation is informed by *The Acts of the Apostles* where three Ananiases appear. In Kitto's *Cyclopaedia of Biblical Literature* (1852), a source Melville apparently used,[49] the first Ananias listed is the Pharisee high priest in Judaea A. D. 48–53. Just as Claggart charged Billy with plotting mutiny, so Ananias charged that Paul was "a mover of sedition . . . and a ringleader of the sect of the Nazarenes" (*Acts* 24:1–5). When Ananias presided at Paul's trial in Jerusalem, Paul prophesied that Ananias would be struck by God: "The high priest Ananias commanded them that stood by him to smite [Paul] on the mouth. Then said Paul unto him, God shall smite thee, *thou* whited wall" (*Acts* 23:2–3). *Acts* does not reveal Ananias's fate, nor does Kitto, but according to Smith's *Bible Dictionary*, which was available to Melville in 1884, Ananias was "assassinated" in the Jewish war.[50]

A second Ananias was the Jewish disciple who led Paul to become the Lord's "witness" (*Acts* 22:12–15); he became bishop of Damascus and, according to Smith, "died by martyrdom" in his own church.[51] If he used Smith's book, Melville would have seen that Smith, like all good propagandists, slants his words so that the first Ananias (the Pharisee priest and *enemy* of Paul) was "assassinated," while the second Ananias (the disciple and *friend* of Paul) "died by martyrdom."

The third and most controversial Ananias was a Christian who lied to Peter; Smith says when Peter exposed him, Ananias "fell down and expired." The narrator of *Acts* implies that Ananias's own guilt caused his death (*Acts* 5:3–5). However, Kitto reports a shocking rumor: "unbelievers have accused Peter of cruelly smiting Ananias"; he also suggests that Peter killed Ananias while at the same time denying the rumor's validity by identifying its perpetrators as "unbelievers."[52] This ironic turn of the screw is exactly how Melville handles the navy report at the end of *Billy Budd*, where victim and culprit are reversed.

IV

The surgeon thinks the captain is "unhinged," but Vere's "passionate interjections" typify the subjectivity associated with any traumatic and controversial event.[53] By viewing Claggart's death as the "divine judgment on Ananias," Vere imposes moral meaning on an inexplicable tragedy. And by seeing Billy as "an angel of God," Vere transforms his already intended execution of Billy into a sublime act of "divine" justice, believing the "angel" will return to heaven. It is what all want to believe when a loved one dies. Vere's revelation is an example of *theodicy* – a vindication of divine goodness in the face of evil or tragedy. It is the process by which Jesus' disciples turned their grief over their leader's death from an unbearable "fact" into joy at the miraculous fulfillment of old prophecies.

Vere's prejudgment that "the angel must hang!" implies his belief in two spheres of being: earthly and heavenly. Vere the military disciplinarian condemns the sailor in the interest of the present or temporal order, while Vere the visionary reassigns an "angel" to the eternal or mystical order. Billy shall be acquitted at "the Last Assizes," Vere tells the tribunal (111).

Calling Claggart's malice a "'mystery of iniquity'" (108),
Vere uses Paul's term for the lying presence which he said
the Lord would destroy "with the brightness of his [second]
coming" (*2 Thes*.2:7–8).[54] Rightly or wrongly, even perhaps
self-servingly, Starry Vere's apocalyptic vision connects Billy
with Christ and the Second Coming; thus he justifies his action
on both military and spiritual grounds. When the captain announces the crime and the punishment, the sailors sit still, like a
"congregation of believers in hell listening to the clergyman's
announcement of his Calvinistic text" (117).

   "Like the prophet in the chariot disappearing in heaven and
dropping his mantle to Elisha, the withdrawing night trans-
ferred its pale robe to the breaking day" (122). In this passage,
Melville imitates the mythopoetic process. First, by conflat-
ing two completely separate events in the biblical account of
Elijah,[55] he shows how myth appropriates material and ar-
ranges it to suit its own artistic purpose. Secondly, he uses the
trope of night turning to day (that is, grief turning to joy) to
translate the idea of sorrow over death (Elijah's) changing to
joy at the vision of the prophet riding into heaven.[56] Here,
Melville demonstrates how theodicy (or myth, one could say)
works to change dark into light, misfortune into good, loss
into gain. The terrible death of Jesus underwent a similar
metamorphosis: by blending "Hebraic grief" with "Hellenic
cheer," the narrators of the Christian story transformed a
scene of utter tragedy (Jesus's crucifixion) into a cause for re-
joicing (the promise of everlasting life). Thus pain, death and
loss are the catalysts for great art, which in turn can transform a subject's life and even make it immortal.

   Through mystical imagery, Billy's transfiguration is com-
plete. We are told that when Billy "ascended," the sky in the
East filled with "a soft glory as of the fleece of the Lamb of
God seen in mystical vision" (124). Melville uses the phrase

"Lamb of God" to link Billy with Jesus, just as the gospels used "the Lamb of God" and "the man of sorrows" to link Jesus with Isaiah's prophecy: "Who hath believed our report? ... He is despised and rejected of men; *a man of sorrows, and acquainted with grief ... he is brought as a lamb to the slaughter,* and as a sheep before her shearers is dumb, so he openeth not his mouth. . . . He was taken from prison and from judgment. . . . Therefore I will divide him a portion with the great" (*Isa.* 53:1–12; my emphasis). "Who hath believed our report?" echoes the evangelist (*John* 12:38), in order to show the fulfillment of prophecy in Jesus. From a heretic and lawbreaker, Jesus was transformed into Isaiah's mute "lamb" and "man of sorrows," the epitome of Hebraism, upon whom the iniquity of mankind was laid.

In *The Confidence-Man* Melville had created the mute man in cream colors as an ironic "Christ-like persona."[57] Similarly here, Melville makes inarticulate Billy an avatar of Jesus and other heroes in order to overturn the navy's account of Billy and "divide him a portion with the great" (*Isa.* 53:1–12). A common sailor who committed the "most heinous of military crimes" (103) is thus transformed into a hero whose death was "phenomenal." He is venerated by "superstitious" sailors who regard each chip of his spar like "a piece of the Cross" (127, 131). The ballad, written by an "artless" sailor of Billy's own watch, shows an ordinary sailor who is sorry he will miss the next "drum roll to grog" (131–32). But the Handsome Sailor has already taken form in readers' minds, and few know of the older gunner in Melville's original manuscript, who had confessed, "My little game is up" before he died.[58] Melville has successfully transformed, or reformed, Billy into the Handsome Sailor.

"But aren't it all sham?" asks Billy at the end, which was once the tale's beginning. It is a moot question for Melville,

who could "neither believe, nor be comfortable in his unbelief," as Hawthorne observed in 1856.[59] By 1891, Melville had
still not tired of the issue of the Bible's relationship to art,
truth, and nature. His final narrative suggests his conviction
that great art need not be literally true to fact, nor indeed can it
be, but on deeper and far more important levels, art expresses
the most profound truth. The actual Billy, like the literal Jesus
or any mythic figure, never existed as the superhuman figure
who has evolved through art, the Handsome Sailor we think
we know. Like classical myth or the Bible, Melville's narrative transforms facts too raw or painful for most readers:
for a beloved young man to die is hard to accept under any
circumstances, as Melville's family knew too well; but if the
young man becomes an "angel of god" honored in heaven and
on earth, the terrible grief over the loss of the beloved one is
assuaged with hope, and the mourners are consoled. This is
the function of Theodicy, which puts a positive face on tragic
events, helping us to accept them. This too is an important
value of great art, such as the Greek myths, the stories of
David in the Old Testament, and the gospels in the New
Testament. As one critic has perceptively argued, the narrative of *Billy Budd* remains "another white lie."[60] Yet Melville's
own religious belief is unclear and his position on the "truth"
of Christianity, in relation to its worth, remains equivocal.

The dialogue between the surgeon and the purser illustrates
opposing views of the Handsome Sailor's superhuman nature.
As to the "absence of spasmodic movement" at Billy's hanging,
the accountant regards it as a "species of euthanasia" or a
kind of miracle. The doctor, representing the rational or scientific perspective, remains skeptical: "*Euthanasia*, Mr. Purser,
is something like your *will power:* I doubt its authenticity as a
scientific term. . . . It is at once imaginative and metaphysical —
in short, Greek" (125). Metaphysics, including the belief in a

world beyond, in a happy afterlife, and in the godhood of Jesus, are all Greek contributions to Christianity. Here again, Melville weighs both sides of such issues.

v

The myth of Billy Budd evolves through the art of language. Similarly, the story of Jesus was for Melville a blend of "legend, dream, and *fact* of life," as the despairing misanthrope says in *Clarel*.[61] Like the New Testament, the "inside narrative" about Billy contains errors, gaps, inconsistencies, ironies, and ambiguities. Nevertheless, as Melville shows, an artful tale transcends historical "fact" to become larger and more powerful than bare truth. According to Northrop Frye, great myths are "the opposite of 'not really true,'" for a myth is "designed ... in a way that does not restrict its significance to that one situation. Its truth is *inside* its structure, not outside."[62]

Melville regarded the Bible as myth, and myth as the highest art. For him, the works of Homer, Milton, Shakespeare, and Hawthorne belonged with the Bible as repositories of the "divine" word. In "The Hero as Poet" (Sealts no. 123), which Melville apparently read while he was writing *Moby-Dick*,[63] Thomas Carlyle wrote that Shakespeare was "a blessed heaven-sent Bringer of Light" and that Jesus too was a poet: "Our highest Orpheus walked in Judea, eighteen hundred years ago." With Carlyle and his American disciple Ralph Waldo Emerson, another of those who stimulated his thought, Melville believed that the true poet was as much a demi-god as Orpheus or Jesus. This was the company to which Melville aspired. In "Hawthorne and His Mosses," as Herbert has pointed out, Melville had likened the "true artist" to Jesus Christ.[64] After *Moby-Dick*, he wrote to

Hawthorne, "In me divine magnanimities are spontaneous and instantaneous. . . . I would sit down with you and all the gods in old Rome's pantheon. . . . Knowing you persuades me more than the Bible of our immortality. . . . The divine magnet is on you, and my magnet responds."[65]

Billy Budd is both a retrospective and a prophetic work. As Sealts has said, this tale "sums up the thought and art of Melville's last years but also looks back in setting, characterization, and theme over his writing as a whole."[66] Although *Billy Budd* grew out of Melville's life experiences, his reading, and his thought, other sources include the 1841 affair of the brig *Somers*, which became a cause célèbre when Midshipman Philip Spencer, son of the United States Secretary of War, was one of three executed at sea without a court-martial for plotting mutiny. Melville was aboard the *United States* at the time he first heard of the affair, but later heard the "inside" story from his cousin Guert Gansevoort, an officer of the tribunal that decided Spencer's fate.[67] Captain MacKenzie's harsh sentence was supported in the press by James Fenimore Cooper, but the public sympathized with the boy. The question of Spencer's guilt remained controversial. Like the English conspirator Guy Fawkes, Philip Spencer became a cult figure, toasted annually even today at Annapolis by young naval cadets.[68] In defense of Captain MacKenzie, Philip Spencer was said to be a known troublemaker, and evidence against him included a note in Spencer's own hand, supposedly "scribbled in Greek,"[69] a factor alluded to obliquely in *Billy Budd* in the dialogue between the surgeon and purser (125).

The character of Billy Budd is informed by many figures, real and mythic, and these include not only the author's two sons but Herman Melville himself. In Billy-in-the-Darbies' original words, "My little game is up,"[70] Melville confessed his own iconoclasm, reprising what he had admitted to Hawthorne in 1851: "I have written a wicked book and feel spotless as the lamb.[71] Billy and Claggart – the "lamb" and the "man of sorrows" – are elements of Melville's artistic vision. Billy represents joy, energy, lyricism, good will, the stylistic qualities that charmed audiences in Melville's early works; in the nineteenth century, many of these qualities were associated with Hellenism's love of beauty and pleasure. In a more specific sense, the Handsome Sailor possesses the "strength and beauty" of *Moby-Dick*, and the tale repeats again Melville's daring assault on the authority of scripture and its creature, the church. As finally portrayed, Billy did not intend satire in his good-bye to the *Rights of Man* nor did he mean to kill the master-at-arms. Melville was not so innocent. But by the 1890s Melville's iconoclasm, his assault on orthodoxy, was forgotten: in America he was identified with *Typee* and its simple charms, while in England men of his watch followed the pieces of his spar.

Claggart is a complex representation of Melville's sense of evil, guilt, Calvinistic sin, "blackness." On the right hand, the master-at-arms is the Hebraic voice, the guardian of the moral good, such as, for example, the Christian press that defended the missionaries from the assaults against them in *Typee* and especially *Omoo*, as well as the righteous critic who attacked *Moby-Dick* as a dangerous book. But on the left hand, Claggart is a part of Melville – the cunning writer of that "wicked" book and the devil's advocate in *The Confidence-Man*. He also exhibits Melville's dark outlook in his middle years, when he denigrated optimism, geniality, the pleasured life, the "good news" of the gospels, and even the charms of his own early works. John Claggart is both the wicked sinner and also the man-of-sorrows upon whom iniquity is unfairly laid; he is both Melville and not-Melville.

Vere is the executor whose judgment is necessarily severe for the good of the whole, at the expense of the individual. "'With mankind,' [Vere] would say, 'forms, measured forms, are everything; and that is the import couched in the story of Orpheus with his lyre spellbinding the wild denizens of the wood'" (128). The "forms" that to Vere are "everything" are both a severe distorter of truth and an essential force in creating lasting art. Vere's allegiance, like Melville's own, is not to Nature, but to the "King," not to physical reality, but to the Eternal. In Starry Vere's cabin, light and dark converge; by imposing form on chaos, Vere does what the writer must do in executing his art: sacrifice the natural and the personal in favor of less perishable meaning. Melville similarly sacrifices the original "rude" Billy-in-the-Darbies, who may have been closer to natural truth, in favor of the Handsome Sailor who, when severely executed, will endure as an heroic ideal. In endowing Billy with heroic form, Melville gives his tale a "moral nature" in keeping with its "comeliness and power" (44).

Innocence and guilt are interchangeable depending on the perspective of one's time and place. Christians, originally persecuted as "atheists" and "outlaws," by the fifth century had become the persecutors of non-Christians, heretics, and iconoclasts.[72] In their own time, the Puritan descendants of John Calvin executed dangerous witches, but from today's perspective they were themselves the real demons. Fame and infamy have likewise been reversed, as with Socrates, Jesus, and other dangerous radicals.

In 1857 Hawthorne had recorded that Melville had "pretty much made up his mind to be annihilated," and, shortly before beginning *Billy Budd*, Herman read that statement in Julian Hawthorne's book.[73] From one point of view, *Billy Budd* addresses that statement attributed to Melville, whether he was referring to the mortality of his soul or of his literary reputation. The naval chronicle's report of Billy as "criminal" can be seen as Melville's last ironic comment on what passes for truth in this world. But irony also mediates the opposite view: Melville may have projected his belief in his own immortality; for in spite of his crime, he survives as the Handsome Sailor in the minds of the tars who follow his mast and perpetuate his legend, as well as in the minds of all who read the "inside narrative."

In *Billy Budd* Melville continued to pursue the protean shape of truth. Like the "moonshine" that enters Billy's cell in the ballad, art's light changes the nature of truth. Beneath the surface of Melville's well-executed tale, *Billy Budd* is a composite of truths and lies – like all immortal Art.

NOTES

1 Herman Melville, *Correspondence*, ed. Lynn Horth (Evanston and Chicago: Northwestern University Press and The Newberry Library, 1993), p. 192. Melville made this statement in his famous "dollars damn me" letter, written to Hawthorne in June, 1851 and published in Julian Hawthorne, *Nathaniel Hawthorne and His Wife*. 2 vols. (Boston: Osgood, 1885). The book (Sealts No. 244) was a gift to Melville from his wife shortly before he began *Billy Budd*, according to Merton M. Sealts, Jr., *Melville's Reading* (Columbia: University of South Carolina Press, 1988), p. 131.

2 Melville, *Billy Budd, Sailor (An Inside Narrative)*, ed. Harrison Hayford and Merton M. Sealts, Jr. (University of Chicago Press, 1962), p. 103. I am grateful to Professor Sealts for his comments on earlier versions of this paper.

3 Hayford and Sealts's "Editors' Introd." explains the stages of composition; their "Genetic Text" shows Melville's revisions.

4 Hayford and Sealts, "Editors' Introd.," *Billy Budd*, 3–4.

5 Lyon Evans, Jr., "'Too Good to be True': Subverting Christian Hope in *Billy Budd*," *New England Quarterly*, 55 (1982): 323–53. Evans believes the tale parodies the gospels.

6 René Girard, *The Scapegoat*, trans. Yvonne Freccero (Baltimore: Johns Hopkins University Press, 1986), pp. 77, 80–82; Girard's emphasis.

7 Stanton Garner, "Fraud as Fact in Herman Melville's *Billy Budd*," *San Jose Studies*, 4 (1978): 82–105. Garner sees the many nautical errors in the tale as evidence of Melville's "pungent irony."

8 Ham saw Noah drunk and naked and told his brothers. Noah cursed Ham, saying Ham's son Canaan would be a "servant of servants . . . unto his brethren" (*Gen.* 9:25–27). Melville satirized America's treatment of the people of Hamora in *Mardi*, ed. Harrison Hayford et al. (Evanston and Chicago: Northwestern University Press and The Newberry Library, 1967). In "Benito Cereno" Melville's double irony shows both sides of the slavery issue, but the symbolism indicates his sympathy lay with the "mutineers." "Benito Cereno," in *The Piazza Tales and Other Prose Pieces*, ed. Harrison Hayford et al. (Evanston and Chicago: Northwestern University Press and The Newberry Library, 1986), pp. 42–117.

9 Charles Anthon, *A Classical Dictionary* (New York: Harper, 1852), p. 103. The dictionary (Bercaw No. 16) went through many editions. Mary Kay Bercaw, *Melville's Sources* (Evanston: Northwestern University Press, 1987).

10 Melville's two sons had already died when he began *Billy Budd*. Cohen and Yannella discuss the effects of Melville's Calvinistic upbringing upon his son Malcolm and its ties with *Billy Budd*. Hennig Cohen and Donald Yannella, *Herman Melville's Malcolm Letter: "Man's Final Lore"* (New York: Fordham University Press and The New York Public Library, 1992), pp. 69–92. See also Laurie Robertson-Lorant, *Melville* (New York: Clarkson Potter, 1996), p. 595.

11 Anthon, 597.

12 Melville's print of Turner's *Apollo Slaying the Python* (A267) is in the Berkshire Athenaeum collection, catalogued in Robert K. Wallace, "Melville's Prints and Engravings at the Berkshire Athenaeum," *Essays in Arts and Sciences*, 15 (1986): 59–90. For an analysis of both Apollo and the Antinous, see Gail Coffler, "Classical Iconography in the Aesthetics of *Billy Budd*," in *Savage Eye: Melville and the Visual Arts*, ed. Christopher Sten (Kent State University Press, 1991), pp. 257–76.

13 A chest of secreted swords turns the compass, wrecking the ship in the Timoneer's story in Melville's *Clarel*, ed. Harrison Hayford et al. (Evanston and Chicago: Northwestern University Press and The Newberry Library, 1991).

14 Melville, "Statues in Rome," in *The Piazza Tales and Other Prose Pieces*, 403, 408.

15 From the 1865 Bohn edition, Cowley translation. Hayford and Sealts, "Notes," 143. Bercaw No. 483 and Sealts, *Melville's Reading*, 75.

16 Anthon, 514 (Bercaw No. 16) calls the fabulous Fabian history "trifling and childish in the extreme." Another Fabius, the Roman consul, used a do-nothing or "Fabian policy" against Hannibal's attacks on Rome; though much criticized, the delay was ultimately successful.

17 Sealts, *Melville's Reading*, 131, and Walter Bezanson, "Melville's Reading of Arnold's Poetry," *PMLA*, 69 (1954): 365–91.

18 "Hebraism and Hellenism" was published in Matthew Arnold, *Culture and Anarchy* (New York: Macmillan, 1867; 1883). In *Robert Elsmere*, called "the finest religious novel of the Victorian Age," two sisters represent Hebraism and Hellenism, while Elsmere unites the two traditions, according to Stephen Prickett, "'Hebrew' vs 'Hellene' as a Principle of Literary Criticism," in *Rediscovering Hellenism*, ed. G. W. Clarke (Cambridge University Press, 1989), pp. 151–53. In Melville's tale a similar antithesis between Claggart and Billy is resolved in the character of Vere.

19 Walter Bezanson, "Historical and Critical Note" in Melville, *Clarel*, p. 587. The present essay is influenced by my reading of *Clarel* and by Bezanson's discussions.

20 *Clarel*, "Historical and Critical Note," 631.

21 Arnold, *Culture and Anarchy*, 135–36.

22 David's slaying of Goliath presaged greatness but also further violence; David became king when his men killed Saul and all his sons; David also arranged Uriah's death in order to take Bathsheba.

23 Matthew Arnold, *Literature and Dogma* (New York: Macmillan, 1873), p. xvi.

24 Claggart has a "strange" beardless chin; his features are *not* actually Greek but merely "cleanly cut as those on a Greek medallion" (64).

25 Hayford and Sealts note the connection, 154.

26 *Omoo*, ed. Harrison Hayford et al. (Evanston and Chicago: North-western University Press and The Newberry Library, 1968), pp. 179–80; my emphasis.

27 The Pharisees' extreme vigilance against non-observance of religious law precipitated the rise of heretical sects. The Gospels report that the Pharisees delivered Jesus to Pilate.

   To protest severe laws against Catholicism, Fawkes plotted with other Catholics to blow up Parliament. Their plan was foiled and the conspirators were hanged; Fawkes became the scapegoat for English Protestant hatred of Catholics.

28 Arnold, *Literature and Dogma*, 18–19, x.

29 Given translations over time, this Plato is hardly "authentic"; "natural depravity" was a phrase unknown to ancient Greeks.

30 Paul warned, "[T]he mystery of iniquity" shall cause some Christians to "believe a lie" (*2 Thes.* 2:7–12). In *Clarel* Melville referred to Paul's "mystery of iniquity" in Canto II.xxxv, "prelusive" to the canto "Sodom."

31 Melville's reading of Hawthorne and its effect on him is discussed in T. Walter Herbert, Jr., *Moby-Dick and Calvinism: A World Dismantled* (New Brunswick: Rutgers University Press, 1977), p. 70. The passage in "Hawthorne and His Mosses" is also cited in Lawrance Thompson, *Melville's Quarrel with God* (Princeton University Press, 1952). Thompson contends that Melville's "deeply rooted" Calvinism led the author to believe that its dogma was "ridiculously true, tragically true," p. 361.

32 *Piazza Tales*, 540–41; my emphasis.

33 Melville joined All Souls Unitarian Church in New York City in 1885 or 1886. Unlike Calvinists, Unitarians were not required to accept any creed: Melville "could be a free spirit . . . and come to his own conclusions." Walter Donald Kring, *Herman Melville's Religious Journey* (Raleigh, N.C.: Pentland Press, 1997), p. 138.

34 Herman Melville, *Collected Poems*, ed. Howard P. Vincent (New York: Hendricks House, 1947), p. 231; my emphasis.

35 *Collected Poems*, 506.

36 *Clarel*, 587–604.

37 *Clarel*, I:28:28–36.

38 W. R. Browning, *Oxford Dictionary of the Bible* (New York: Oxford University Press, 1996), p. 266. Jesus is the Latin form of the Greek word for the Hebrew name Joshua or Jehoshua; Christ is the Anglicized form of Christos which is Greek for the Hebrew word "messiah," meaning "anointed one"; Browning, 199 and 6.

39 *Moby-Dick*, 424; my emphasis.

40 *Correspondence*, 212; my emphasis.

41 *Correspondence*, 209; my emphasis.

42 Jay Leyda, *The Melville Log* (New York: Gordion, 1969): 1:437.

43 Herman Melville, *The Confidence-Man*, ed. Harrison Hayford et al. (Evanston and Chicago: Northwestern University Press and The Newberry Library, 1984), p. 136.

44 *The Confidence-Man*, 239, 243; my emphasis.

45 *The Confidence-Man*, 243.

46 Joseph was sold to the Ishmaelites (*Gen.* 37:28).

47 A vestal served the Roman hearth goddess Vesta; she was buried alive if she broke her vow of chastity (Anthon, 1379–80).

48 *Collected Poems*, 231.

49 Bercaw No. 421. John Kitto, *The Popular Cyclopaedia of Biblical Literature, Condensed from the Larger Work* (Boston: Gould and Lincoln, 1845; 1852). Melville apparently used Kitto's book when writing *Clarel*. Bezanson, "Historical Note," 704.

50 William Smith, *A Dictionary of the Bible* (Philadelphia: Henry T. Coates, 1884), p. 39.

51 Smith, 39.

52 Kitto, 67.

53 In *Clarel*, "religious traditions are not branded as delusions . . . but as personal, subjective illusions," according to Stan Goldman, *Melville's Protest Theism* (Dekalb: Northern Illinois University Press, 1993), p. 114.

54 For a discussion of "mystery of iniquity" see note 30.

55 The prophet Elijah cast his mantle upon his successor while Elisha was plowing, but this occurred shortly after Elijah forecast the downfall of King Ahab, long before Elijah's death (*1 Kings* 19:19).

56 See *Psalms* 30:5; Browning, 268.

57 Jonathan Cook, *Satirical Apocalypse: An Anatomy of Melville's "The Confidence-Man"* (Westport, Conn.: Greenwood, 1996), p. 85.

58 Hayford and Sealts, "Genetic Text," 277.

59 Hawthorne's *Journal*, November, 1856 (Leyda, 2:529).

60 John Samson, *White Lies: Melville's Narrative of Facts* (Ithaca, N.Y.: Cornell University Press, 1989), p. 211.

61 *Clarel*, 3.28:17.

62 Northrop Frye, *The Great Code: The Bible and Literature* (New York: Harcourt, Brace, 1982), pp. 33, 46; my emphasis.

63 Thomas Carlyle, "The Hero as Poet," in *On Heroes, Hero-Worship and the Heroic in History* (New York: Scribner's, 1896–1901).

64 Herbert, 71.

65 *Correspondence*, 212–13.

66 Sealts, "Innocence and Infamy: *Billy Budd, Sailor*," in *A Companion to Melville Studies*, ed. John Bryant (Westport, Conn.: Greenwood, 1986), p. 407.

67 Hayford and Sealts, "Editors' Introd.," 28–30. See also Hershel Parker, *Herman Melville* (Baltimore: Johns Hopkins University Press, 1996), I:242, where he presents evidence that Elisha Small, one of Spencer's coconspirators, was part of the inspiration for *Billy Budd*.

68 *The Curse of the Somers, Billy Budd's Ghost Ship*, Documentary Film. Written and Directed by George Belcher. Project Limited Partnership, 1995.

69 Robertson-Lorant, 120.

70 Hayford and Sealts, "Genetic Text," 277.

71 *Correspondence*, 212.

72 Ramsey MacMullen, *Christianizing the Roman Empire: A.D. 100–400* (New Haven: Yale University Press, 1984), pp. 54, 101.

73 Julian Hawthorne, 2:135.

3

Old man Melville: the rose and the cross

Robert Milder

> . . . how live
> At all, if once a fugitive
> From thy own nobler part, though pain
> Be portion inwrought with the grain?
> — Melville, *Clarel*[1]

In this chapter I would like to take for granted the rich body of commentary on the political, philosophical, mythological, and religious meanings of *Billy Budd* and to ask a different sort of question: what did it mean for Melville at the end of his life to spend close to six years writing and revising *Billy Budd*? He began the narrative early in 1886; expanded and recast it over the next two and a half years; undertook to put it in fair-copy form in November 1888 on the assumption that it was finished; then resumed work on it again, more than doubling its length and refocusing its subject, and continued to revise and polish it, sometimes with important thematic consequences, until his death in September 1891.[2]

Though by far the most familiar of his late writings, *Billy Budd* was one of four substantial projects that engaged Melville after his retirement from the New York Custom House in December 1885, and, as Hershel Parker observes, it "needs to be seen in relation" to this other contemporaneous work – the verse collections *John Marr and Other Sailors* (1888), *Timoleon* (1891), and "Weeds and Wildings" (posthumous

1924) – rather than "as the single obsessive labor of Melville's last lustrum."[3] "Obsessive" is misleading so far as it implies all-consuming attention, yet it is hard to imagine how else to characterize Melville's apparent "inability to let the story go"[4] at a time of declining physical and mental energy and sometimes outright pain. *Billy Budd* meant something special to Melville, not only because it marked his belated return to fiction but because, as a story that unfolded as he worked on it, it prompted *him* to unfold in ways that even the best of the late poetry did not.

Readers looking to *Billy Budd* for Melville's deathbed "testament" usually focus on matters of political or religious belief. These are among its preeminent concerns, certainly; but when we situate the narrative within the body of Melville's late writing, particularly beside his other unpublished manuscript, "Weeds and Wildings," the issue raised by its long and complicated genesis is not so much what to believe – about God or nature or society – as how to conduct oneself amidst the uncertainties of belief. "I did not care what it was all about," Hemingway's Jake Barnes remarks in *The Sun Also Rises*: "All I wanted to know was how to live in it. Maybe if you found out how to live in it you learned from that what it was all about."[5] Melville never ceased caring what life was all about, but unable to fathom it either by intellect or by faith he increasingly came to feel that living "aright" was the closest one might come to grasping its meaning. The question that occupied him particularly in his last years was whether to commit himself to this world or the next, with the latter understood not simply as a problematic immortality or an equally problematic literary immortality but as everything comprehended under the word "spirit" and ranged against the claims of physical sense. Or was this opposition factitious? Could sense and spirit be harmonized, so that to live with a refined aesthetic hedonism was simultaneously to live for the soul? In a poem from "Weeds and Wildings" titled "The New Rosicrucians" Melville envisions a latter-day order of philosophers whose talismanic symbol is the Rose-Vine twined round the Cross. Was late Meville himself a "New Rosicrucian"? What did the rose mean for him? What had the cross come to mean? And is the twining, or failure to twine, of these organizing symbols a key to whatever putative "testament" may be found in his late work?

I

Exempt from [malice], in blest recline
  We let life's billows toss;
If sorrow come, anew we twine
  The Rose-Vine round the Cross.
  – Melville, "The New Rosicrucians"[6]

"The New Rosicrucians" is one of eleven rose poems in "Weeds and Wildings," a collection of pastoral verse whose aura of repose led Newton Arvin to speak of "the unprotesting tranquillity that Melville achieved at the end of his life."[7] In truth, many of the pastorals in "Weeds and Wildings" were contemporaneous with the bleak nautical poems of *John Marr* and intended for an inclusive volume provisionally titled *Meadows and Seas* (Ryan vii). The "tranquillity" of "Weeds and Wildings" is a triumph of genre and thematic occasion, yet like the very different tones of *John Marr*, *Timoleon*, and *Billy Budd*, it corresponds to an element in the larger configuration of mind and mood we imaginatively reconstruct as "Old Man Melville."

Outwardly, Melville's tranquillity was secured by a reclusiveness that led him to spurn attempts to bring him forward into the literary world of New York and, as admirer Arthur

Stedman observed, to avoid "speak[ing] of himself, his adventures or his writings in conversation."[8] Forgotten himself, Melville worked to develop the art of forgetting, down to telling a visitor (disingenuously) that "he didn't own a single copy" of his books.[9] A "hermit" to his contemporaries,[10] Melville projected his situation in the poem "The Garden of Metrodorus" from *Timoleon*:

> The Athenians mark the moss-grown gate
> And hedge untrimmed that hides the haven green:
>   And who keeps here his quiet state?
>   And shares he sad or happy fate
> Where never foot-path to the gate is seen?
>
> Here none come forth, here none go in,
> Here silence strange, and dim seclusion dwell:
>   Content from loneness who may win?
>   And is this stillness peace or sin
> Which noteless thus apart can keep its dell?

Melville knew Metrodorus from (among other sources) Schopenhauer's *The Wisdom of Life*, which he read in 1891 and which alludes to Metrodorus as a disciple of Epicurus who titled one of his chapters, "*The Happiness we receive from ourselves is greater than that which we obtain from our surroundings.*"[11] Schopenhauer's subject is "the art of ordering our lives so as to obtain the greatest possible amount of pleasure and success" (Schopenhauer 1), a theme much on Melville's mind after 1885, when the opportunities of leisure along with flagging energies and ill health combined to pose again the question of how to live. In "The Rose Farmer," the climactic poem in "Weeds and Wildings," Melville's narrator, an elderly man who like himself has "come unto [his] roses late," seeks advice about whether to harvest the rose for enjoyment or profit or with difficulty to press its petals into attar. How should a man of leisure comport himself within his garden, an area of peace cordoned off from the world yet inviting a languor that may, in some sort, be "sin"?

The serenity of the garden was all the more enticing for the harshness that lay outside it. Had Melville published *Meadows and Seas* in the form he envisioned almost to the last, it would have turned upon the contrast between a small, enclosed, and largely benign rural world and an immense and pitiless oceanic one. As it is, the short "Sea Pieces" in *John Marr* – "The Aeolian Harp," "Far Off-Shore," "The Figure-Head," "The Berg," "Old Counsel," and "Pebbles," among others – comprise a summary statement of Melville's metaphysics: youth is headstrong and naively optimistic, nature treacherous, and life a tale of literal or figurative shipwreck. "Healed of my hurt, I laud the inhuman Sea," the speaker of "Pebbles" manages to conclude, but the backdrop of nature in *John Marr* is so alien to "The hope of [man's] heart, the dream in his brain" that a foreground of human meaning and value, at the very least of stoic indifference, needs to be constructed as a bulwark against it.

Even when it is not explicitly present in Melville's late writing, the "blank sea," as Melville would call it in *Billy Budd* (*BB* 61, 109), is the ontological reality against which any viable philosophy must be judged. *Timoleon* is a more miscellaneous volume than *John Marr*, but in a sequence of poems beginning with "The Garden of Metrodorus" Melville frames the question of how to live in a naturalistic world in terms of a conflict between aspiration and worldly compromise, solitude and society, spirit and flesh. At one extreme is the alluring sensualism of "Lamia's Song" ("Descend, descend! / Pleasant the downward way –/ From your lonely Alp . . . "), at the other the transcendent idealism of "The Enthusiast" ("Though light forsake thee, never fall/ From fealty to light"), replicated in the triumphs or spiritual fidelities of the artist-seekers of

"The Weaver," "In a Garret," "Lone Founts," "The Bench of Boors," and "Art."

The "rose" and the "cross" are both absent from *Timoleon*, but the poems' alternatives of worldly pleasure and unworldly striving had been the values attached to the rose and the cross, respectively, since *Clarel*. The young Cypriote in *Clarel* is Melville's portrait of the rose-worshipper at his most prepossessing, if naive ("'With a rose in my mouth/ Through the world lightly veer:/ Rose in my mouth/ Makes a rose of the year!'" [*C* III, 4:129]); the merchant from Lesbos, "light and rosy" (*C* III, 26:71), his example of rose-religion grown coarse with age. The cross is linked to believers or would-be believers like Salvaterra and the Syrian Monk, but it is also associated with the soldier Ungar, the doubters Celio and Mortmain, and the quester Rolfe. The distinguishing mark of the cross is not Christianity *per se* but an earnestness of mind and temper that shows itself in what Salvaterra calls "'the pure disdain/ Of life, or holding life the real,/ Still subject to a brave ideal'" – "'The habit of renouncing, yes'" (*C* IV, 14: 34–36, 39). Walking the Via Crucis at the end of the poem, Clarel sees common suffering humanity as "Cross-bearers all" (*C* IV, 34:43), but there is also the "rarer quest" that labors under "so much more the heavier tree" (*C* IV, 34:47–48), and this is the cross of an aspiration that will never, if it looks honestly at experience, be rewarded by belief but will preserve nonetheless an intensity of inward life that is itself a vindication of "*the spirit above the dust*" (*C* IV, 35:11), whether or not immortality proves to be a fact.

By the time of the late poetry, Melville had modified his notion of the rose and its relation to the cross, partly because he had become a rose gardener himself, literally and metaphorically, and partly because his reading had acquainted him with a more sophisticated aesthetic hedonism. Among the books that affected him most was Anglican clergyman Samuel Reynolds Hole's *A Book About Roses*, a genial, discursive celebration of the rose and rose gardening somewhat in the manner of Ishmael's celebration of the whale intermixed with elements of a floral Art of Courtly Love.[12] Melville read Hole for instruction and delight, but he would also have been sensible to the presiding image of the garden as an enclave of order and serenity, created by art, labor, and love, that went as far toward repairing the Fall as sublunary efforts could. "The Rosarium," Hole wrote of the rose garden in a passage Melville marked, "must be both exposed and sheltered; a place of both sunshine and of shade. The center must be clear and open, around it the protecting screen. It must be a fold wherein the sun shines warmly on the sheep, and the wind is tempered to the shorn lamb; a haven in which the soft breeze flutters the sails, but over which the tempest roars, and against whose piers the billow hurls itself, in vain."[13]

"Weeds and Wildings" is Melville's Rosarium, a pastoral realm of peace and unassuming beauty fenced off from the importunities of the social world and the naturalistic grimness of Creation, which nonetheless hovers around the edges of the volume and is suggested by one of its cancelled epigraphs, "Alms for Oblivion." To achieve happiness by rejecting "the aspiring mind" is "the central meaning of pastoral" with its ideal of "*otium*," a "state of content and mental self-sufficiency."[14] In his gentle, affectionate dedication "To Winnefred" (his wife Lizzie), Melville seems almost to have reached this state as he eulogizes the humble red clover, a favorite flower of Lizzie's, in place of the wild amaranth, here as in *Pierre* a symbol of aspiration and immortality. Within what might be called the Darby-and-Joan interpretation of "Weeds and Wildings," Lizzie is "the ideal reader to whom the poems are addressed"[15] and the collection is an extended love letter, or act of reparation for marital difficulties, or simply a testament to "the companionable ease of husband and wife who have grown old together."[16] Yet Lizzie seems the recipient only of the light rustic poems of Part I ("The Year"), which recall early days at their Pittsfield farm; and as the volume unfolds, culminating in the rose poems, it grows in depth, reflectiveness, and authorial self-reference in a way that the non-literary Lizzie might have admired but scarcely understood.

The closing poems of "A Rose of Two" measure the limits of the pastoral garden as Melville presses the symbol of the rose to discover whether it can, or should, yield spiritual attar. In "The Rose Window" the speaker falls asleep in church during a "homily" on the resurrection and dreams of "an Angel with a Rose" shedding red light on "the shrouds and mort-cloths" of the dead. Has the speaker bypassed formal religion and arrived, via the rose (suggestive of the Virgin Mary's rose?), at a visionary faith? We can't be sure. The dead, though ruddily illuminated, remain as stolid as "the meek members of the Resurrection" who wait endlessly and perhaps futilely in Emily Dickinson's "Safe in their Alabaster Chambers."[17] All that is certain is the pageant of color the speaker sees upon awakening – dust motes transfigured by the roseate light streaming through "the great Rose-Window high." One may read the poem, with John Bryant, as illustrating "the power of faith, beauty, art, and the rose to transfigure matter into spirit,"[18] or one may read it in the opposite way as implying that immortality is conjectural at most but the glories of sense experience palpably real. "Which is best?" Emily Dickinson asked in one of her countless variations on this theme, "Heaven –/ Or only heaven to come/ With that old Codicil of Doubt?" – "The 'Bird within the Hand'" or the one that may – "or may not" – be in "the 'Bush'"? (#1012)[19]

As if in answer to this question, "Rosary Beads" finds its heaven in the succession of intense perceptual moments:

> Adore the Roses; nor delay
> Until the rose-fane fall,
> Or ever their censers cease to sway;
> "To-day!" the rose-priests call.

More than any other poem of Melville's, "Rosary Beads" borrows the rituals of Christianity to deck the secular hedonism of "that sublime old infidel,"[20] Omar Khayyám, whose *Rubáiyát* Melville owned in three copies. "After vainly endeavouring to unshackle his steps from destiny, and to catch some authentic glimpses of TO-MORROW," as translator Edward FitzGerald wrote in a preface Melville marked, Omar "fell back upon TO-DAY (which has outlasted so many tomorrows!) as the only ground he had got to stand upon, however momentarily slipping from under his feet."[21] For the Sufi poets, as Dorothee Finkelstein noted, "the traditional Persian imagery of wine, roses, and love became a code of mystical symbols" in which intoxication and the "contemplation of beauty" were seen as routes to the divine.[22] Similarly, Whitman, a poet who interested Melville deeply in the 1880s and who had affinities with Sufi mysticism, found an unorthodox but not unspiritual rosary in "the glories strung like beads on my smallest sights and hearings."[23] Sense perception, gauzily idealized, could itself become a bridge between the natural and the supernatural for those wary of conventional theology or determined simply to have the best of both worlds. "Omar was too honest of heart as well as of head for" such "cloudy symbolism," FitzGerald remarked (Fitzgerald 7). So was Melville, who admired in Omar the same unillusioned sense of transience and ultimate oblivion he found in Ecclesiastes, and who in "Rosary Beads" adapted the language of Christian miracle (transsubstantiation) to an aesthetic hedonism whose rewards were of the temporal world: "But live up to the Rose's light,/ Thy meat shall turn to roses red,/ Thy bread to roses white."

Among the books Melville seems not to have read – surprisingly, given his interest in art and philosophical epicureanism – was Walter Pater's *The Renaissance* (1873), in which the flux of experience is seen in terms of an organic vitalism more throughly naturalistic than Whitman's yet endlessly rich in its phantasmagoria of aesthetic impressions. "Not the fruit of experience [what Melville would call the "attar"], but experience itself, is the end," Pater wrote: "A counted number of pulses only is given to us of a variegated, dramatic life. How may we see in them all that is to be seen in them by the finest senses? How shall we pass most swiftly from point to point, and be present always at the focus where the greatest number of vital forces unite in their purest energy?"[24]

"Rosary Beads" imagines a Paterian harvesting of the moment, but its affirmation is blighted by the encroachment of time and death, as "Grain by grain the Desert drifts/ Against the Garden-Land." Intimations of mortality in Melville almost invariably dash the Paterian dream of "treat[ing] life in the spirit of art."[25] Responding to an 1888 request from Edmund Clarence Stedman for an autograph version of "one of your best known shorter poems" for a projected anthology (*Correspondence* 738), Melville replied with the obscure "Ditty of Aristippus," a rose poem sung by the Cypriote in *Clarel* about the revels of the immortal gods. "The Rose by their gate/ Shall it yield unto fate?/ They are gods –/ They are gods and their garlands keep green" (*C* III, 4:11–14). But is the rose sufficient for those who are not gods and whose perpetuity lies in cultivating a very different flower, the amaranth? So Vine asks in the lyric he recites during the revels at the monastery Mar Saba, as if in answer to the sanguine Derwent's song about the rose-worshipping Sufi poet Hafiz (*C* III, 13:71–80). Vine counters: "'The rose-leaves, see, disbanded be –/ Blowing, about me blowing;/ But on the death-bed of the rose/ My amaranths are growing'" (*C* III, 14:35–38). "'*His amaranths*,'" Vine adds scornfully of the Florentine artist from whom he heard the poem: "'a fond conceit,/ Yes, last illusion of retreat'" (*C* III, 15:39–40). For Vine a rose-garden is a rose-garden and not, as for the Sufis or the "New Rosicrucians," a ladder to heaven.

Transcendence or non-transcendence is the issue Melville addresses in what John Bryant calls "his blockbuster conclusion" to "A Rose or Two" (Bryant 64), "The Devotion of the Flowers to Their Lady." The poem is about the Fall, the experience of "banishment," and the "secret desire/ For the garden of God" even amidst the pleasure garden of the world. The rose worshipped temporally for its beauty becomes, in the closing lines of the poem, a "voucher" of immortality, but the conclusion is forced upon the subject by its ascribed author, an eleventh century Provençal troubador who, like the Sufi poets, sought to pass by way of symbolism from the profane to the sacred, only to renounce "Love and the Rose" later in life and retire to a monastery, as if in acknowledgment of the discontinuity between heaven and earth. The poem recalls Samuel Reynolds Hole's pronouncement in *A Book about Roses*, "What is our love of flowers, our calm happiness in our gardens, but a dim recollection of our first home in Paradise, and a yearning for the Land of Promise!" (Hole 105). As a rose gardener and a clergyman, Hole likes to imagine horticulture as a running lesson in "the truths of Revelation, the histories and prophecies of the Older Testament, [and] the miracles and parables of the new" (Hole 104); but finally Hole must concede, as Melville does in "The Devotion," that "our gardens do not satisfy, are not meant to satisfy, our heart's desire" (Hole 106). Though Bryant sees the theme of the poem as "Paradise Regained . . . through beauty and the rose" (Bryant 64), Melville's emphasis falls rather upon loss ("Ah, exile is exile though spiced be the sod"), with heaven residing only problematically, as for Dickinson, in "the 'Bush.'"

Despairing of finding God either in nature or in a monastery, Melville might have contented himself with the literal and poetic rose-garden he shared with Lizzie. Yet aside from being wholly terrestrial, a pastoral refuge could also be enervating. By the shift of a single consonant and a corresponding shift in attitude, *otium* (content) might slip easily into *odium* (hatred), the Latin root that, according to Reinhard Kuhn, lies behind the word "ennui."[26] From the early Middle Ages onward, Kuhn observes, ennui "on the one hand . . . designated something, often of a petty nature, that proved vexatious and irritating" and, "on the other hand . . . a profound sorrow" or "deep spiritual distress" (Kuhn 5, 6) – scarcely the paradox it seems, since existential feelings often have roots in mundane domestic ones. John Bryant's characterization of Lizzie as "patien[t] beyond any deep understanding of [Melville's] art and anxiety" (Bryant 50) seems, intentionally or not, to mingle praise for Lizzie's unswerving fidelity to a man she perceived as great with criticism of her exasperating obtuseness toward the things he most deeply cared about. Perhaps it is this ambivalence that accounts for the cloying archness of the dedication "To Winnefred," reminiscent of the early pages of *Pierre* and suggesting a hidden disparagement of pastoral serenity and possibly of Lizzie herself.

"Mere leisure, that is to say, intellect unoccupied in the service of the will, is not of itself sufficient," Schopenhauer wrote," . . . for as Seneca says, *otium sine litteris mors et vivi hominis sepultura* – illiterate leisure is a form of death, a living tomb" (Schopenhauer 5). A leisure productive of "Weeds and Wildings" is hardly "illiterate," but neither did pastoral verse or the tranquillity it celebrated nurture the feeling of aspiration Melville had in mind when he pasted to a sidewall by his desk, out of sight to all eyes but his own, "a printed slip of paper that read simply, 'Keep true to the dreams of thy youth.'"[27] "These dreams," granddaughter Eleanor Metcalf commented, "grew out of the deepest needs of the whole man" and "reflected a desire to nourish the roots of life. . . . In other words, they were religious in nature" (Metcalf 284). In "The Rose Farmer" the elderly speaker neglects the advice of "Rosary Beads" ("Adore the Roses, nor delay . . . ") as he weighs the claims of the rose and the attar, Pateresque sense experience versus whatever of art or truth or self-transfiguration might be expressed from it. True, the Persian rose-farmer concedes, "'the redolence [of the moment] stales./ And yet you have the brief delight,/ And yet the next morn's bud avails;/ And on in sequence'" – "'This evanescence is the charm!/ And most it wins the spirits that be/ Celestial'" – by which he means, it lures "the sons of God below" to the "fugitive" charms of earth, much as "the downward way" in "Lamia's Song" woos lonely mountaineers to "myrtles in valleys of May."

Although the speaker of "The Rose Farmer" lauds the Persian for "sapient prudence not amiss" (equivocal words in Melville's vocabulary), the poem ends without a visible commitment. Melville's own career did not. Readers of "Weeds and Wildings" who see "Melville's late vision of art and life as 'play'"[28] understimate how far even his lighter poems are achievements of disciplined will. "Essential Oils – are wrung," Emily Dickinson said: "The Attar from the Rose/ Be not expressed by Suns – alone –/ It is the gift of Screws" (number 675). Melville's own metaphor for creation in the poem "Art" is "wrestl[ing] with the angel," a fit image for the laborious struggle that shows even in the manuscript revisions of this eleven-line poem.[29] Writing came hard for the elderly Melville – it was an art of screws – and precisely for this reason it served him, in lieu of Christian belief, as a "cross." I do not mean that Melville arrived at a religion of art or that, as William B. Dillingham says, "at times, [his] treatment of artistic inspiration so resembles a description of religious experience that the two are virtually indistinguishable" (Dillingham 91). Creation for Melville was not at all like religious experience, if one means by that an exalted and quasi-mystical intuition of the suprarational. Rather, art was akin to vital religion so far as it involved living on the stretch and refusing to accede to the claims of the natural man, an austerity that extended down to the "carpetless room, gloomy and monastic in appearance,"[30] in which he wrote. Melville was not an ascetic; his attention simply turned inward as art became the medium for a spiritual life focused on the self's effort continually to exceed its boundaries against the downward pull of age and sickness and the allure of rest. "Whilst we converse with what is above us" – not God, but the next level of our own being – "we do not grow old, but grow young," Emerson wrote.[31] It is pleasant to imagine Old Man Melville redeemed from the struggles of life by Christian faith, marital love, or the "blest recline" of the "New Rosicrucians," but struggle (the "cross") was the last thing he wanted to be redeemed from, for struggle was itself redemptive in the Emersonian sense of ever-rejuvenating. So, among other things, Melville may have implied when he prefaced "Weeds and Wildings" with an epigraph adapted from Hawthorne's *Dolliver Romance*: "Youth is the proper, permanent, and genuine condition of man" (Ryan 1).

II

A man wants to use his strength, to see, if he can, what effect it
will produce. . . . From this point of view, those are happiest of all
who are conscious of the power to produce great works animated
by some significant purpose.

– Schopenhauer, *Counsels and Maxims* (704–05)

Billy Budd is Melville's consummate work of screws and a
record of his final growth. The book began modestly with
the poem "Billy in the Darbies," a sailor monologue of the
sort Melville would publish in *John Marr.* From there the
manuscript unfolded through what editors Harrison Hayford
and Merton M. Sealts, Jr., describe as "nine major stages of
inscription with their substages" (HS 239), continuing nearly
to his death. In expanding and revising the narrative, Melville
dramatized incidents he originally had only reported; he reas-
signed a number of authorial opinions to fictive characters; he
worked toward greater precision of statement and at the same
time toward calculated ambiguity; and he shifted the thematic
focus of the tale, most notably after November 1888 (when
he thought the manuscript was complete) by developing the
characterization of Captain Vere and adding the trial and execution scenes. Even at the last, he reworked manuscript leaves
in pencil, changing words and passages throughout and sub-
stantially altering the role of the surgeon in a way that throws
unsettling crosslights on Vere and opens his behavior to ironic
interpretation. There is no telling how, if at all, he might have
harmonized his materials had he lived; possibly he would have
done very little: the thrust of his revisions was toward ever
greater complication and multiplicity of perspectives. In any
case, the manuscript he left behind is the product not of a single controlling intention but of successive intention*s*, and one

whose significance as an index to late Melville lies less in its attitudes at any particular point than in the journey of mind visible in and through its evolving emphases and transmutations of word and phrase.

Billy Budd joins the rose and the cross in the hanging scene when the "pinioned" (crucified) Billy ascends and takes "the full rose of the dawn" (*BB* 124). The question is what this convergence means – specifically, whether its religious idiom is allegorical or figurative. Has Melville come to an otherworldly faith in the transcendent? to a reconciliation of heaven and earth? or to an understanding of "heaven" as the rarest and most exalted of earth? To suggest that *Billy Budd* is about the "Fall" and "Redemption" is not *ipso facto* to constrain Melville within the Christian scheme, but to ask how he recasts Christian myth to express his particular sense of the natural and the spiritual.

Melville linked Billy with the rose from his first description of the "lingeringly adolescent expression" in Billy's face, "where, thanks to his seagoing, the lily was quite suppressed and the rose had some ado visibly to flush through the tan" (*BB* 50). In an earlier draft of the passage "visibly" was absent and the rose had "much [not 'some'] ado" to show itself. The effect of Melville's revision is to highlight the rose as the inward moral component of Billy's "rose-tan" (*BB* 77, 119), outwardly stained by the weathering of sun and wind. Billy's rose complexion is a pastoral analogue to his associations with Adam, Hercules, an "upright barbarian" (*BB* 52), and "a dog of St. Bernard's breed" (*BB* 52), versions of good-natured but pre-intellectual and pre-societal being. Even the name of the ship from which Billy is impressed, the *Rights-of-Man*, suggests a pre-societal order, whether of the savage Hobbesian sort (a state of internecine war, as it was before Billy's coming) or of the pastoral Rousseauean sort (a benign fraternal anarchy, as it became under Billy's influence). In either case, Melville intimates that a "natural" state will not suffice. "Ethically," as Hallett Smith remarked, pastoral ". . . is always vulnerable to the objection that virtue can consist only in action" in the turbulent citified world; "from Aristotle to Milton there is always some stern voice which announces, 'I will not praise a cloistered virtue'" (Smith 57). In *Billy Budd* that voice is the Dansker's with his "grim internal merriment" (*BB* 70) and premonition of catastrophe; it is Claggart's with his "disdain of innocence – to be nothing more than innocent!" (*BB* 78); and it is the narrator's when, echoing Milton's "Areopagitica," he calls Billy a "child-man" whose innocence is not far removed from the child's "blank ignorance" (*BB* 86). In opening his story, moreover, with the figure of the "Handsome Sailor" – leaves written *after* his initial characterization of Billy in what became Chapter 2 (HS 244, 275) – Melville chooses to introduce Billy ironically in terms of what he is not, a "champion" and "spokesman" of the crew (*BB* 44).

The insufficiency of innocence was a theme in *Billy Budd* virtually from its inception, but in the narrative of 1888 the primary focus was upon Claggart (Vere was only incidentally mentioned as the officer who condemns Billy; the trial and execution scenes were as yet unwritten) and the thematic emphasis was largely theological. The story was a reenactment of the myth of the Fall that morally exonerated its child-like Adam and arraigned God for his accountability for evil (Claggart in his malice is "like the scorpion for which the Creator alone is responsible" [*BB* 78]). Melville never expunged this early context of (anti-)Christian allegory, but he did outgrow it as his quarrel with God exhausted itself and his interest passed to the public world of history and politics and subsequently to the private world of what he called "certain phenomenal men" (*BB* 75; HS 333). Christian imagery appears in this later material as well, but the point of reference is no longer Christian and the language functions more as a resonant gloss on characters and events than as symbols within an articulated religious parable. The story's cosmic backdrop is now thoroughly naturalistic – "the monotonous blank of the twilight sea" (*BB* 109), against which the characters must live and act without appeal to the transcendent – and its central subject is the tragedy of governance, with Vere from one perspective an anguished but duty-bound servant of the political state, from another a myopic conservative whose punitiveness reflects the larger society's system of repression.

None of these concerns had been present to Melville when he began the tale. Two magazine articles on the *Somers* incident of 1842, the first appearing in the spring of 1888, may have kindled his memory of his cousin Guert Gansevoort, an officer aboard the *Somers* when an acting midshipman and two sailors were hanged for conspiracy, and prompted him to brood on issues of justice, natural rights, and social order. Yet having raised these matters, Melville found them challenging him, first, to crystallize his thoughts on political justice, then, unexpectedly, to *de*-crystallize them as his subject began to unfold in its seemingly inexhaustible complexity.

Manuscript evidence suggests that Melville composed a substantial portion of the trial and execution scenes before he interpolated the character analysis of Chapters 6 and 7 that established Vere as a Burkean conservative of a peculiarly inward and idiosyncratic sort – bookish, prone to dreamy gazing "at the blank sea" (*BB* 61), and with "'a queer streak of the pedantic'" (*BB* 63). Melville's political themes were in place, that is to say, before he began exploring the roots of judgment in Vere's individual cast of mind and temper. Chapters 6 and 7 by no means discredit Vere's arguments in the trial scene, but they do contextualize them in a way that makes them utterances of a particular man in a particular historical circumstance rather than universal and authorially sanctioned truths about God's law and man's. If the composition of the trial scene turned *Billy Budd* from theological allegory to political meditation, Melville's additions concerning Vere had the effect of redirecting the story once again, this time toward psychology, or politics as refracted through psychology. Hershel Parker has argued that Melville's late pencil revision of the surgeon's role – the surgeon's belief that Vere may be "unhinged" (*BB* 102) and that Billy's case should be referred to the admiral – contradicts what had been an earlier authorial endorsement of Vere (Parker 174). The changes do introduce a far more measured, ambiguous, and at points markedly critical attitude toward Vere, but the process of qualification began almost as soon as Melville conceived Vere as a distinct personality.[32] Politics required political actors, and once the actors became more than mouthpieces for opinions they assumed a dramatic interest that increasingly absorbed Melville in its own right.

Surveying *Billy Budd* as a thematically sequential text, one can describe its long gestation as a movement upward from anecdote ("Billy in the Darbies") to theological myth (the 1888 manuscript), then downward to the particularized world of human affairs in which there were no certainties and no universal truths, only the spectacle of single and sometimes singular individuals acting within the crush of circumstances and under the manifold pressures of history, culture, and conscious and unconscious disposition. In *Pierre* (1852) Melville had observed that no mind "ever arrives [at] an earthly period, where it can truly say to itself, I have come to the Ultimate of Human Speculative Knowledge; hereafter, at this present point I will abide."[33] The achievement of *Billy Budd* is in converting the absolutist's chagrin at the elusiveness of truth into a stimulus for ever-deepening inquiry. Instead of "covertly pack[ing]" the cards of his fictional deck, as Pierre comes to believe all writers disingenuously do (*Pierre* 339), Melville works to unpack them by pushing further to the *next* level of insight (Vere's psychology), even if it means ironically qualifying, even subverting what had formerly seemed to him "the truth."

An art premised on the creed that "truth uncompromisingly told will always have its ragged edges" (*BB* 128) appeals to a standard not of aesthetic harmony, but of scrupulousness, or perceptual and linguistic fidelity to the object at hand. "The great aim" of art, T. E. Hulme remarked, is "accurate, precise and definite description,"[34] wrought with pains against the resistance of habitual modes of observation and the conventionalisms of language and technique. The artist trying to represent what he sees is like a man exerting his entire force to bend "a springy piece of steel" out of its received shape into "the exact curve" he wants (Hulme 133). Hulme wrote as a champion of Imagism trying to "prove that beauty may be in small, dry things" (Hulme 131). *Billy Budd* shows that this almost muscular concentration of mind – Dickinson's "art of screws"; Melville's "wrestl[ing] with the angel" – also applies to larger things and may be consonant with an *a*-"symmetry of form" (*BB* 128) that proceeds from the author's evolving engagement with his material.

Such an asymmetry is hardly unprecedented in Melville's writing. Except in the magazine pieces of 1853–56 – "Bartleby, the Scrivener," "Benito Cereno," and a few of the other tales – formal unity had never been a characteristic of Melville's fiction, largely because of his habit of acceding to what Warner Berthoff called "that rush of interior development which served him for education."[35] The dislocations of *Billy Budd* differ from those of *Mardi*, *Moby-Dick*, and *Pierre* in that they were not prompted by an intellectual or emotional growth originating outside the text so much as by a sense of beckoning possibilities *within* the text. The lesson of the manuscript evidence is that *Billy Budd* grew by metamorphosis as Melville discovered new frameworks of understanding *and* that it became increasingly detailed, nuanced, capacious, and problematic as he gave himself to communicating as much of the truth of an intricate and broadly ramifying human situation as could be imaginatively grasped and verbally rendered. At each point he worked with the intensity of the Hulmian miniaturist, but his enclosing structure of sequential emphases took its shape from something nearer to the Emersonian principle "that around every circle another can be drawn" and that in art, as in nature, "there is no end . . . , but every end is a beginning" ("Circles" 179). The history of the narrative shows Melville's extraordinary fictive ambition at a time when the very act of living had become increasingly difficult; yet more than that, it suggests his determination to try the limits of his being and, in lieu of any definite belief in otherworldly transcendence, to enact his commitment to the "cross" – "'holding life the real,/ Still subject to a brave ideal'" (*C* IV, 14:35–36) – through a life of continual *self*-transcendence.

This relocation of the spiritual within the temporally human is the key to whatever religious "testament" *Billy Budd* has to make, whether through its characters and action or as its development reflects the pilgrim's progress of its author. When Melville speaks of Billy on the scaffold as "spiritualized now through late experiences so poignantly profound" (*BB* 123), he is not referring to a transformation of the "natural" Billy into a literal or figurative Christian. Billy remains to the end a "barbarian" (*BB* 120) unresponsive to the chaplain's gospel of "salvation and a Saviour" (*BB* 121), yet within the terms of his character he has been deepened by suffering – Captain Vere's, perhaps, even more than his own. His final words, "God bless Captain Vere!" (*BB* 123), are his naturalistic *imitatio Christi*, or intuitive version of "'the chronometrical gratuitous return of good for evil'" (*P* 215) that Melville regarded as the distinguishing moral characteristic of Christianity. Melville is not symbolically associating Billy with Christ; he is setting aside the theological substance of Christianity and invoking its nimbus (as in the "soft glory" that "chanced" to illuminate "the vapory fleece hanging low in the East" during Billy's execution [*BB* 124]) to suggest the power of tragically doomed individuals to rise above their fate in remarkable acts of magnanimity. "Most men," says Faulkner's Ike McCaslin in *Go Down, Moses*, "are a little better than their circumstances give them a chance to be."[36] Late Melville would probably have amended "most men" to "certain phenomenal men," but for him, too, spirituality was a quality of sublunary life nurtured by suffering and displayed in acts of generosity, compassion, high integrity, and sacrifice.

Crucial to Billy's development is the closeted interview in which Vere communicates the sentence to him and is open about his own role in effecting it. If Vere's "cross" – "the agony of the strong" (*BB* 115) perceptible in his face as he leaves the compartment – is to bear the weight of a decision he knows is tragically unjust, Billy's "cross" is emotionally to perceive and honor the pain of his captain, which he cannot intellectually begin to understand. For readers reluctant to allow that Melville can empathize with Vere at all, the "quasi-liturgical language" of the scene, as Laurie Robertson-Lorant called it, may seem a "particularly offensive kind of moral casuistry" assignable to the story's narrator rather than to Melville himself.[37] The compositional evidence indicates otherwise. The Billy who originally might only "have *discerned* the brave opinion of him" implied by Vere's frankness is elevated in the late pencil revision to one who "might have *appreciated*" it, or taken its symbolic measure, while Vere "the *monkish* devotee of military duty" becomes, more respectfully, "the *austere* devotee" who "may in end have caught Billy to his *heart*" rather than, as formerly, "to his *arms*" (HS 440; emphasis added; *BB* 115). In contrast to the general movement toward irony and authorial distance in the late revisions, Melville's changes in Chapter 22 work to solemnify the scene by cultivating a language, religious in mood but not in literal content, commensurate with his feeling of admiration toward the human.

The revisions that ennoble Billy and Vere individually also combine to show them "as bound to one another in a complementary greatness of soul" (Berthoff 199) for which the union of the rose and the cross is, in a non-theological sense, a fit image. On one side, the closet scene "subverts what the author saw as the traditional Christian view of salvation and modifies it with a reverence for Eros (frequently symbolized by the rose)";[38] on the other, it transmutes spontaneous, untutored Eros through the sanctifying agency of grief, commonly symbolized by the cross. Just as Billy redeems Vere by softening him and evoking the father beneath the social disciplinarian, so Vere redeems Billy, whose moral juvenility, like the roundness of his cheek, is burned away by the anguish he feels himself and witnesses in Vere. Billy's dying words, unimaginable without "the something healing in the closeted interview" (*BB* 119), indicate his debt to Vere, while Vere pays homage to Billy in his own dying words, "'Billy Budd, Billy Budd,'" uttered, Melville is careful to report, in "accents" other than those of "remorse" (*BB* 129). Melville has not twined the rose around the cross in the sense of joining pastoral earthiness and Christian transcendence. His "rose" is the essential substratum of joy and peace and goodness in man, his "cross" the spiritualizing reagent of struggle and pain that (with Billy) transfigures the natural into the exaltedly human and (with Vere) dissolves the layers of artifice to restore hypersocialized man to his emotive being.

No world beyond the terrestrial is required or supposed here, though neither is it excluded. "The meek, shy light [that] appeared in the East" (*BB* 122) on the morning of Billy's execution may or may not intimate a presiding divinity; cognizant only of what Melville elsewhere called "the visable truth" (*Corr* 126), we, like the sailors on the *Bellipotent*, cannot be certain. Nor can we extract from the relationship of Billy and Vere a consoling model for social reorganization that would obviate future tragedy. Society in our "ponderously cannoned" (*BB* 124) world proceeds as it will, and whatever triumph Billy and Vere achieve individually and through each other belongs to them as particular beings and occurs within the fixities of institutional blundering and cosmic silence. Melville has not reconciled himself to God or society, but neither is he angrily hurling himself against them. Rather, in the last months of his life he has come to focus on the grandeur men can attain for themselves despite (or sometimes because of) the misprisions of earth and the indifference of heaven.

In light of this concern with grandeur, it is significant that in presenting the closet scene Melville should have reversed his compositional thrust toward dramatization and offered it as "a speculation so bold and so personal as to be all but indistinguishable from fantasy" (Parker 145). Eloquent in its reserve, the chapter hints at depths and sanctities scarcely to be grasped by the imagination or entrusted to the public medium of language. But the chief effect of Melville's technique is to call attention to the origin of the scene in the narrator's sensibility, so that the greatness of Billy and Vere ultimately attests to the generosity of his own spirit. "Fantasy" the scene assuredly is, but fantasy is what we are known by, both at our worst (the fantasies generated by the unconscious) and at our best (the fantasies of our self-ideal).

To write sublimely of sublime behavior is on some level to inhabit the elevated fictive world and share in emotions and states of being as removed from mundane experience as a Latin mass from the din of the street. For the non-believer, particularly, literature may become the scene for a spiritual life unrealizable within the terms of religion or the actional possibilities of experience. Reading Mme. de Staël's *Germany* years earlier, Melville boxed and checked her remark, "Poetic genius is an internal disposition, of the same nature with that which renders us capable of a generous sacrifice."[39] The writer is like the magnanimous hero by the very nature of his activity, the imagination calling forth in him the nobility of character that crisis evokes in the man of events. Forgotten by his American audience, Melville needed continually to reassure himself of this. In revising the digression on Lord Nelson (Chapter 4), he altered the phrase "good enough peradventure for varlets" (a propos of the introduction of firearms as an inglorious replacement for swords) to "good enough peradventure for peasants," then finally to "good enough peradventure for weavers" (HS 304; *BB* 56) – the last suggesting not only sedentary craftsmen but, as in Melville's poem "The Weaver," lonely and austere artists. Could the writer, by any stretch of the imagination – that is to say, by any arduous work of self-transcendence – become the associate or equal of the sacrificing hero? Melville seems to answer this question covertly for himself at the end of the Nelson chapter when, defending the "priestly motive" that led Nelson at Trafalger "to dress his person in the jewelled vouchers of his own shining deeds," he likens the assumed magnificence of the naval hero to the grandiloquence of the high mimetic writer: "if thus to have adorned himself for the altar and the sacrifice were indeed vainglory, then affectation and fustian is each a more heroic line in the great epics and dramas, since in such lines the poet but embodies in verse those exaltations of sentiment that a nature like Nelson, the opportunity being given, vitalizes into acts" (*BB* 58). To celebrate in writing the behavior of a Nelson, a Billy Budd, or a Vere was, for Melville, to enact a kindred heroism, outward opportunities in the writer's case *not* being given.[40] Heroism's mark in literature as in action was a splendor of bearing and "its jest," in Emerson's words, "the littleness of common life,"[41] as Melville implied when he deprecated the "martial utilitarians" (*BB* 57) who accused Nelson of vanity and opposed his behavior to prudence and calculation.

Nelson is not a Christian hero for Melville. His sign is the "star" inserted in his ship's quarter-deck on the spot where he fell in battle (*BB* 57). And perhaps the star is the true emblem for what Melville imagined as the metamorphosis of the natural man (the rose) via aspiration and suffering (the cross) into a spiritual being even within the context of temporal life, which is the only context an agnostic can be sure of. In this respect, Nelson's warship, the *Victory*, could not have been more aptly named. The same might be said for "'Starry Vere,'" a lesser man than Nelson and without "brilliant" qualities yet distinguished from his peers by an earnest, ruminative cast of mind (*BB* 61). In the Epilogue to *Clarel* Melville had presented "the running battle of the star and clod" (*C* IV, 35:16) as the condition of living in a seemingly godless world. He never ceased to hope that in historical time or after death some revelation of the divine might be granted. Until then, men defined themselves as belonging figuratively to heaven or earth by how they behaved, and critical to their behavior – the virtual test of grace for Melville – was the intensity with which they gave themselves to the struggle for truth.

As Melville's final texts, "Weeds and Wildings" and *Billy Budd* are complementary works of the imagination, just as for the living writer they must have been complementary places of emotional residence. In the aesthetic hedonism of "Weeds and Wildings" Melville found much to admire and still more to enjoy. Yet even at its most philosophical, pastoralism with its repose entailed an accommodation to the earth and in that respect was antithetical to the star. The "blest *recline*" of "the New Rosicrucians" – an inclining *backwards*, as the word literally suggests, "blest" only in the sense of "pleasurable" – signified the regression to a more elementary or indifferent psychic state that renounced aspiration and made light of the spiritualizing medium of sorrow. Melville's characteristic posture, reaffirmed by the compositional history of *Billy Budd* as well as by its progression of themes, was the upright one memorialized in a poetic paraphrase of lines from Book V of the *Aeneid* translated for him in 1877 by his admiring brother-in-law John C. Hoadley:

> Drawing the shaft
> Until its feathers touch his swelling breast,
> Its barb his out-stretched hand, he aims
> Full at the veiléd stars. Shrill twangs the string,
> The singing arrow flies, a gleam of light
> Athwart the blue, like a resurgent star
> Restored to heaven where the Mantuan bard
> Hath bid it shine for aye. The highest aim
> Hath won the highest prize.
>
> Aim high and do your best:
> Then, though the mark be hid, the generous deed
> Shall ever shine, – itself the highest prize.
>
> (*Corr* 716–18)

NOTES

1 Herman Melville. *Clarel: A Poem and Pilgrimage in the Holy Land*, Ed. Harrison Hayford, Alma A. MacDougall, Hershel Parker, and G. Thomas Tanselle (Evanston and Chicago: Northwestern University Press and The Newberry Library, 1991), IV, 28: 81–84. Hereafter cited in the text as *C*.

2 For an account of the composition of *Billy Budd*, see Harrison Hayford and Merton M. Sealts, Jr., "Editors' Introduction," in *Billy Budd, Sailor* (University of Chicago Press, 1962), pp. 1–12. All references to *Billy Budd* as well as to editorial matter by Hayford and Sealts will be to this edition and will be included in the text and abbreviated as *BB*.

3 Hershel Parker. *Reading "Billy Budd"* (Evanston, Ill.: Northwestern University Press, 1990), p. 32.

4 John Wenke. "Complicating Vere: Melville's Practice of Revision in *Billy Budd*," *Leviathan*, 1 (1999): 83.

5 Ernest Hemingway. *The Sun Also Rises* (New York: Scribners, 1957), p. 152.

6 Editions of the manuscript "Weeds and Wildings" are problematic. Howard P. Vincent included the collection, with errors and arguable editorial judgments, in his edition of *Collected Poems of Herman Melville* (Chicago: Packard, 1947), but until the appearance of the Northwestern-Newberry edition of the unpublished manuscripts, the most reliable text (and the one to be cited in all references of "Weeds and Wildings") is Robert C. Ryan's "'Weeds and Wildings Chiefly: With a Rose or Two,' by Herman Melville. Reading Text and Genetic Text, Edited from the Manuscripts, with Introduction," Dissertation Northwestern University Press, 1967.

7 Newton Arvin. *Herman Melville* (New York: William Sloane, 1950), p. 280.

8 Arthur Stedman. "Marquesan Melville," in Merton M. Sealts, Jr., *The Early Lives of Melville* (Madison: University of Wisconsin Press, 1974), p. 106.

9 O. G. Hillard, quoted in Jay Leyda. *The Melville Log* (New York: Harcourt Brace, 1951), p. 787.

10 See Merton M. Sealts, Jr. *The Early Lives of Melville* (Madison: University of Wisconsin Press, 1974), pp. 20–28.

11 Arthur Schopenhauer. "The Wisdom of Life," in *The Pessimist's Handbook: A Handbook: A Collection of Popular Essays by Arthur Schopenhauer*, trans. T. Bailey Saunders, ed. Hazel E. Barnes (Lincoln: University of Nebraska Press, 1964), p. 4. All references to Schopenhauer will be to this edition of *The Pessimist's Handbook*.

12 For a fine discussion of Melville and Hole and of Melville's symbolism of the rose generally, see William B. Dillingham. *Melville and His Circle* (Athens: University of Georgia Press, 1996), pp. 140–75.

13 Samuel Reynolds Hole. *A Book About Roses* (New York: William S. Gottsberger, 1883), p. 56.

14 Hallett Smith. *Elizabethan Poetry* (Cambridge, Mass.: Harvard University Press, 1966), p. 10.

15 William H. Shurr. *The Mystery of Iniquity* (Lexington: University Press of Kentucky, 1972), pp. 183–84.

16 Shurr, "Melville's Poems: The Late Agenda," in *A Companion to Melville Studies*, ed. John Bryant (Westport, Conn.: Greenwood Press, 1986), p. 365.

17 *The Complete Poems of Emily Dickinson*, ed. Thomas H. Johnson (Boston: Little, Brown, 1960), no. 216. Hereafter cited in the text by poem number.

18 John Bryant, "Melville's Rose Poems: As They Fell," *Arizona Quarterly*, 53 (1997): 67. Though Bryant's reading of the rose poems, and of late Melville generally, is quite different from mine, his subtle, imaginative, and thoroughly informed article is among the best discussions of "Weeds and Wildings."

19 Melville would have found an echo of Dickinson's question (and an emphatic answer) in Omar Khayyám's quatrain, "Some for the Glories of This World; and some/Sigh for the Prophet's Paradise to come;/Ah, take the Cash, and let the Promise go,/Nor heed the music of a distant drum." *The Rubáiyát of Omar Khayyám (First and Second Editions) and Six Plays of Calderon*, trans. Edward Fitzgerald (London: J. M. Dent, 1928), 2nd edn., Quatrain XIII.

20 *The Writings of Herman Melville. Correspondence*, ed. Lynn Horth (Evanston and Chicago: Northwestern University Press and The Newberry Library, 1993), p. 497.

21 Fitzgerald. "Omar Khayyám: The Astronomer-Poet of Persia," in *The Rubáiyát of Omar Khayyám (First and Second Editions) and Six Plays of Calderon*, 9.

22 Dorothee Metlitsky Finkelstein. *Melville's Orienda* (New Haven: Yale University Press, 1961), pp. 104, 241.

23 Walt Whitman. "Crossing Brooklyn Ferry," *Leaves of Grass*, ed. Sculley Bradley and Harold W. Blodgett (New York: Norton, 1973), 1. 9.

23 *The Rubáiyát of Omar Khayyám (First and Second Editions) and Six Plays of Calderon*, trans. Edward Fitzgerald, Quatrain LXXX (2nd edn.).

24 Walker Cowen. *Melville's Marginalia* (New York: Garland, 1987), p. 259.

24 Walter Pater. *The Renaissance*, in *Walter Pater: Three Major Texts*, ed. William E. Buckler (New York University Press, 1986), p. 219.

25 Pater, *Appreciations*, in *Walter Pater: Three Major Texts* 428.

26 Reinhard Kuhn. *The Demon at Noontide* (Princeton University Press, 1976), p. 5.

27 Eleanor Melville Metcalf. *Herman Melville: Cycle and Epicycle* (Cambridge, Mass.: Harvard University Press, 1953), p. 284.

28 Lucy M. Freibert. "*Weeds and Wildings*: Melville's Use of the Pastoral Voice," *Essays in Arts and Sciences*, 12 (1983): 66.

29 See Robert C. Ryan. "Melville Revises 'Art,'" in *Melville's Evermoving Dawn: Centennial Essays*, ed. John Bryant and Robert Milder (Kent State University Press, 1997), pp. 307–20.

30 Edwin Haviland Miller. *Melville* (New York: George Braziller, 1975), p. 343.

31 *Collected Works of Ralph Waldo Emerson, Volume II. Essays: First Series*, ed. Alfred R. Ferguson and Jean Ferguson Carr (Cambridge, Mass.: Harvard University Press, 1979), p. 189.

32 HS 309; see Wenke 85–86.

33 Herman Melville. *Pierre; or, The Ambiguities* (Evanston and Chicago: Northwestern University Press and The Newberry Library, 1971) p. 167.

34 T. E. Hulme. *Speculations* (New York: Harcourt Brace, 1924), p. 132.

35 Warner Berthoff. *The Example of Melville* (Princeton University Press, 1962), p. 15.

36 William Faulkner. *Go Down, Moses* (New York: Random House, 1990), p. 329.

37 Laurie Robertson-Lorant. *Melville* (New York: Clarkson Potter, 1996), pp. 591–92.

38 George B. Hutchinson. "The Conflict of Patriarchy and Balanced Sexual Principles in *Billy Budd*," *Studies in the Novel*, 13 (1981): 393.

39 In Cowen 632.

40 By "celebrate" I do not mean that Melville shares or approves of Vere's judgment in the case of Billy but that, however wrong Vere may have been or however swayed in his decision by unconscious factors of temperament or ambition; in Melville's eyes he is elevated by the pain he undergoes and by his mutually ennobling exchange with Billy in the closet scene.

41 Emerson. *Collected Works, Vol. II*, 149. In his copy of Mme. De Staël's *Germany* (inscribed 1862), Melville underlined her observation that "*as we advance in life, purdence gains too much upon all our other virtues*" (Cowen 641).

4

Melville's indirection: Billy Budd, the genetic text, and "the deadly space between"

John Wenke

I

While assembling officers for a drumhead court, Captain Vere includes a marine and "perhaps deviated from general custom." The marine's "judicious" and "thoughtful" attributes make him "not altogether incapable of grappling with a difficult case." Vere, however, is "not without some latent misgiving." An "extremely good-natured man," the marine is "an enjoyer of his dinner, a sound sleeper, and inclined to obesity." A late pencil patch added to the fair-copy inscription further qualifies his character: "though he would always maintain his manhood in battle [he] might not prove altogether reliable in a moral dilemma involving aught of the tragic."[1] The immediate impression of Vere's approbation dissolves: To be "not altogether incapable" makes one not quite capable. Perhaps Vere has grounds for reservation. But then again, one wonders, why is Vere, conservative champion of "forms, measured forms" (Chap. 27, leaf 333), deviating from custom in the first place?

This revised passage signals the critical complexities attending *Billy Budd*, especially insofar as it depicts competing claims to interpretive authority. The narrator may be presenting Vere's prescient distrust of his supposed coadjudicators or his invidious tendency toward narrow self-righteousness. Is

Captain Vere the just and sane man he believes himself to be, "no lover of authority for mere authority's sake," one loathe to monopolize "the perils of moral responsibility" (Chap. 21, leaf 244)? Or in "[s]o thinking" does he delude himself and thus usurp the prerogative of higher authority – the Admiral, the Natural Law, the Divine Law – by rushing to judgment and summarily executing Billy Budd, "a fellow creature innocent before God" (Chap. 21, leaf 267)? Where do Melville and the narrator stand in relation to these dichotomous, and textually valid, readings?

Like "Bartleby, the Scrivener," *Billy Budd, Sailor (An Inside Narrative)* evokes visceral responses. As Robert Milder puts it, *Billy Budd* "taps commitments of ethical, political, and philosophical value that make its criticism peculiarly confessional and urgent."[2] The deeply-felt horror at Billy's death often finds expression in arguments that excoriate or palliate Vere for doing what he (supposes he) had to do. The allegorical conflict between the pristine (nearly perfect) Billy Budd and the infernal (yet deferential) John Claggart establishes the context for ideologically determinate interpretations. Vere's decision to hang Budd for killing Claggart has led critics to assess Melville's intentions as revelatory of either conservative or liberal sympathies.[3] The conservative Melville renders Vere as a humane, thoughtful classicist – a horrified functionary all too agonized over how primal innocence must, in this knot of circumstances, be martyred to insure the stability of "lasting institutions" (Chap. 7, leaf 84).[4] The liberal Melville renders Vere as a complacent, fascistic oppressor – a warship dictator all too eager to slaughter innocence in a calculated display of brutal *realpolitik*.[5] In either case, a fixed metaphysical allegory of good and evil subserves the fixed parable of conservative or liberal politics. Such bifurcated approaches presuppose the existence of an essentially finished text, which contains a

knowable and authorially endorsed point of view – a narrator who stands as a projection of Melville's attitude, whether
conservatively or liberally inclined; or a narrator who functions as an ironic foil, himself a "character," a bumbling, myopic one at that, whose wrongheaded praise for Vere must
signal the author's castigation of Vere.[6] Any particular ideological reading emerges as the culmination of Melville's years
of revision. Thus, while technically unfinished, the narrative
exhibits closure and achieves the iconic status of last artistic
testament, all but signed over to the legatees of posterity.

In *Billy Budd* the witting or unwitting presumption of a fixed
and final text and the attending promulgation of a determinate narrator constitutes a critical fiction that obscures the em-
battled, if not tortured, nature of Melville's actual narrative.
Billy Budd was indeed left nearly finished at Melville's death,
but it had been *considered* fully finished at least three times
before. The genetic text of *Billy Budd*, brilliantly constructed
and analyzed by Harrison Hayford and Merton M. Sealts, Jr.,
and virtually unexamined over the last forty years, does not
present a manuscript but a compilation and collation of successive fair-copy inscriptions, each started with the printer's
eye in mind, each drawing Melville into significant recasting.
Critical arguments that impose ideological or New Critical
cohesion on *Billy Budd* can only do so by concentrating on
evidence within the reading text that seems to validate one's
deductive premise. At best, such arguments refuse to admit the
full range of available evidence and become exercises in the
art, or artifice, of selected self-justification – arguments that
are in themselves political allegories in the form of literary
criticism.[7] The reading text, then, becomes what it is not – an
independent and final product of artistic intention – rather
than what it is – a dependent and conditional outcome
of Melville's arrested compositional process. At worst,
in Hershel Parker's view, critics interested in discussing

Melville's intentions who refuse to base "any of their arguments on the Genetic Text as well as the Reading Text . . . have
often proceeded with analyses which were simply not worth
doing, wrong from the start."[8]

As the genetic text reveals, Melville's shifting intentions,
and the words that reflect them, emerge as part of a complex activity of trial and transformation. Indeed, over five slow years,
Melville was rereading and remaking a text that intrigued,
haunted, and even baffled him. Even in the latest fair-copy
inscriptions – at stages F and G – Melville was not simply tin-
kering with words and phrases but making decisive alterations
that seem *designed* to thwart the determinate readings so characteristic of *Billy Budd* criticism. Through successive stages of
expansion and revision, as Hayford and Sealts argue, Melville
was consistently "*dramatizing* the situation (and its implications) which he had previously *reported*."[9] Consequently, such
dramatizations enact the very events which provide the basis
for Melville's "inside narrative." Rather than functioning as
an unequivocal, completely reliable conduit of information,
the narrator becomes something like a mediator. Melville's
transformation of exposition into dramatization not only cre-
ates the illusion of extrinsic events and circumstances, but it
also limits the range of the narrator's authority. The narrator evidences considerable but by no means complete access
to events and motives. Melville's narrative voice is variously
expressive *and* retentive: He offers what he purports to know
in relation to what he purports not to know. His determinate statements establish boundaries beyond which lie the
shadowland of conjecture. Situated in a dramatic present –
his "now" – the narrator offers an interaction between determinate and indeterminate formulations, a self-conscious
reconstruction of events from "the time before steamships."[10]
At a temporal remove, the narrator describes characters and
recounts incidents. These actors and actions constitute a kind

of text that invites multiple interpretations. In his speculations, in his retentiveness, in his admissions of ignorance, in his presentation of other interpreters and other texts *within* his text, the narrator insistently complicates and frustrates the possibility for forging a determinate reading. Thus, the narrator celebrates an open-ended process of inquiry that accepts the contextual validity – indeed, the epistemological necessity – of approaching the "boggy ground" of historical reconstruction through admittedly provisional formulations. At crucial junctures, for example, he invites the reader to partake of the process of interpretation. How does one approach a "phenomenal" nature like Claggart's? One crosses "the deadly space between" and gives oneself to the dialectical play of imaginative possibility. Is Vere sane? This is a question "every one must determine for himself by such light as this narrative may afford" (Chap. 21, leaf 237).

The fact that *Billy Budd* criticism is replete with polarized arguments does not mean that one camp is right and the other wrong. Rather, the text contains valid and reasonable grounds for numerous positions. Melville scholarship, therefore, should be less concerned with judging Vere than contending with Melville's powerful, perhaps irreducible, dramatization of conflicting imperatives. Melville's indeterminacy is not a matter of relegating meaning to a deconstructive vortex, but a matter of recognizing that language (and events described by language) have an attenuated complexity, representational by nature, that invites mediate pursuits, or assays, after a possible truth, but which eventually become exhausted by that very process. What emerges is not completion or closure but the cessation of a dialectical process.[11] The ambiguity of *Billy Budd* is an essential, functional concomitant to Melville's fictionalized confluence of historical, political, and moral forces as they impinge upon an individual's – Vere's – consciousness and action. As the genetic text reveals, Melville became increasingly preoccupied with constructing a "moral dilemma" if not an interpretive conundrum. The absence of a textually encoded, authorized *Gestalt* does not indicate that *Billy Budd* is incoherent or that Melville's mental powers were failing. Rather, the novel pays homage to, because it depicts, the root uncertainty inherent in the genre of historical fiction. By insisting that his story has "less to do with fable than with fact" and by admitting that "[t]ruth uncompromisingly told will always have its ragged edges," the narrator recounts a "less finished," necessarily incomplete, and possibly more mimetic account of life-as-it-was (Chap. 28, leaf 335). The reconstruction of historical circumstances involves a subtle symbiosis between events-as-lived and the narrator's reconstruction of them, between "fact" and "[t]ruth uncompromisingly told," between extrinsic action and inside narrative.

This essay concentrates on the narrator's performance as reflected not only in the reading text but, more importantly, in selected, representational revisions as documented in the genetic text. Whether one sees the narrator as a dramatic extension of Melville himself or as a dissociated fictional persona, the genetic text reflects Melville's involvement with making and remaking the narrator's tale. In viewing the reading text by such light as the genetic text affords, one can specify distinct choices made by Melville that become reflected in the narrator's words. One can illuminate thereby the nature of the narrator's authority as it emerges in (and conditions) the process and products of interpretation. What becomes most crucial are those points where the narrator's unquestioned determinations about character or action give way to the problematical arena of conjecture, "indirection," and lacunae – this "deadly space between" the fixed products of cause and effect and the political, moral, and metaphysical involutions that make for chartless navigation through the "boggy ground" of the "*might-have-been*" (Chap. 4, leaf 65, Melville's italics).

2

The impressment scene provides a critically unproblemati-cal point of departure. In depicting Billy's transfer from the merchantship the *Rights of Man* to the frigate the *Bellipotent*, Melville in four instances transformed unequivocal, often judgmental, formulations into less determinate, often bland, ones. Taken together, these revisions introduce Melville's tendency toward favoring indeterminate representation and thereby complicating his text's interpretive problem.

Captain Graveling, the narrator observes, spent his entire life "contending with the intractable elements, alike in Nature and man" (Chap. 1, leaf 13). In deleting "alike in Nature and man," Melville displaced allegorical and ontological impli-cations in favor of a flatly naturalistic statement. He down-played Graveling's disciplinarian function. Later, after Billy calls "And good-bye to you too, old *Rights-of-Man*," Melville deleted "kidnapping" from "lieutenant" (Chap. 1, leaf 29) and vacillated in two places over whether Billy breaches naval "decorum" or "discipline" (Chap. 1, leaf 30). By deciding on "decorum," Melville made Billy's "salutation" less trouble-some. Similarly, he altered Billy's "capture" to "impressment" and then to "enforced enlistment" (Chap. 1, leaf 31). In these cases, Melville subverted the invidious figure in favor of neu-tral language, though it could be argued that "enforced enlist-ment" is a sardonic euphemism. The shift from inflammatory to tempered (or possibly satiric) language reflects Melville's decision to efface direct editorial judgment. In so doing, he avoided putting the narrator in overt opposition to the British Crown.

The narrator concentrates instead on delineating the rad-ical disparity between the lieutenant and Billy, between the officer's presumption of Billy's satiric intention and Billy's complete exemption from "double meanings and insinuations" (Chap. 1, leaf 30). In the narrator's view, the ontological anomaly of Billy's primal innocence finds fitting complement in Billy's status as biographical cipher. He neither knows his place of birth nor his parentage. When one of the officers asks, "Do you know anything about your beginning," the narrator depicts Billy's genealogical and ontological mystery.[12] Melville changed Billy's reply that he was found "in a basket of oakum" to a "pretty silk-lined" basket, thus invoking a lost origin of nobility, wealth, and even "a mother eminently favored by Love and the Graces" (Chap. 2, leaves 39–40). The revisions underscore the irresoluble mystery of Billy's "[n]oble descent" and his common lot (Chap. 2, leaf 41).

The narrator depicts the beauty of Billy's nature in light of its essential opposition to the complexity of fallen existence. The "unsophisticated" Billy is exempt from those "moral obliquities which are not in every case incompatible with that manufacturable thing known as respectability" (Chap. 2, leaf 43). Repeatedly, the narrator insists on the intrinsic corruption of artificial constructs. Billy's identification with animal imagery links him not only with the natural primitive, but as "upright barbarian" Billy also possesses typal qualities of the prelapsarian Adam (Chap. 2, leaf 44). Significantly, the narrator's allegorical presentation of Billy appears early in the compositional process (at stage B) and is augmented at D and E, prior to Melville's extensive pencil draft stage (X) when Vere's role was developed. The danger of typal representation is that Billy might remain a flat, one-dimensional icon. Perhaps to modify the typal dimensions, the narrator (at D) points out that there is "just one thing amiss in him," his "occasional liability to a vocal defect" (Chap. 2, leaf 46). It was not until the latest stage of inscription (at G) that Melville developed the implications of Billy's stutter. The narrator

editorializes on the ubiquity of the Fall: "In this particular
Billy was a striking instance that the arch interferer, the envious marplot of Eden, still has more or less to do with every
human consignment to this planet of Earth. In every case, one
way or another he is sure to slip in his little card, as much as
to remind us – I too have a hand here." The narrator insists
on Billy's human status. Coming as it does after Melville inscribed (at F) most of the Vere material, these revisions (at G)
qualify Billy's archetypal status. Melville's revisions have implications regarding genre as well. In a patched addition, the
narrator dissociates his story from "romance": "The avowal
of such an imperfection in the Handsome Sailor should be
evidence not alone that he is not presented as a conventional
hero, but also that the story in which he is the main figure is
no romance" (Chap. 2, leaf 48). As in *Moby-Dick*, Melville
feared that *Billy Budd* would be construed as a "hideous or
monstrous allegory."[13] These revisions seem conditioned by
Melville's presentation of Vere's conflicting imperatives, his
conflict between "primeval" feeling and official duty. Late
in the compositional process, Melville returned to an early
part of the narrative and demythologized Billy (Chap. 22,
leaf 288).

While concerning "the inner life of one particular ship
and the career of an individual sailor" (Chap. 3, leaf 49), the
Bellipotent's drama cannot be dissociated from the contingen-
cies of its historical moment. The Napoleanic Wars in general
and the Nore mutiny in particular provide brutal forces that,
first, create the need for impressment; second, make possible the *Bellipotent*'s imminent engagement with the enemy;
third, make uncertain the loyalty of the "People." In broad
strokes the narrator describes the Nore mutiny as a harbinger
of anarchy. As with the early allegorization of Billy Budd,

Melville depicted contending historical forces through determinate political categories. Melville's struggles were not with
ideas but with precise wording. At first, "the flag of organic law
and right" becomes transformed into "the enemy's red rag of
revolt and universal revolution." At least three versions later,
the narrator describes the mutiny as "transmutting the flag of
founded law and freedom defined, into the enemy's red meteor
of unbridled and unbounded revolt" (Chap. 3, leaf 52). While
favoring "founded law," the narrator admits that "practical
grievances" grew out of "[r]easonable discontent." On the
one hand, the inside narrative seeks to offset the paucity and
distortions of official information and to tell the truth about the
mutiny; on the other, the narrator concludes that the mutiny
was a temporary "irruption of contagious fever in a frame
constitutionally sound." Adding to the divided portrait is the
fact that the mutineers helped "win a coronet for Nelson at
the Nile, and the naval crown of crowns for him at Trafalgar"
(Chap. 3, leaf 56–57). The allegorical material tends to belong
to the earlier stages of inscription. In later stages, Melville did
not displace allegory so much as complicate its rendering with
ambiguous fine shadings. As his revisions progressed, Melville
modified the allegorical dimensions, especially as he considered the vexing impingements of historical circumstances on
the leaders responsible for making decisions and acting upon
them.

    The pertinence of the Admiral Nelson material, especially
in Chapter 4, divides pro- and anti-Vere camps.[14] The issue
concerns the problem of reading Vere through Nelson. Nelson
stands either as a complement or reproach to Vere. The genetic
text does not help resolve this question, though it does indicate
how Melville recognized the troubling nature of the Nelson
material.

The main body of the Nelson material (leaves 62–72) was inscribed at the *B* stage, well before Vere had any role. Nelson was clearly an iconic figure, monumental in proportions. At *D* Melville withdrew the material; at *G*, well after Vere's development, Melville restored the Nelson leaves and introduced them by inscribing three new leaves (58–60).[15] On leaf 58, the narrator announces his detour into "a bypath. If the reader will keep me company I shall be glad." In committing this "literary sin," the narrator *seems* to be marginalizing the Nelson material. The narrator's indirection, however, has a pertinence beyond whether Nelson functions as model or foil for Vere. Identifying himself as writing in a compositional present, the narrator calls attention to, and demonstrates, the problematical narrative negotiation involved in translating an individual's existential action from some time past into the reconstructed text of historical discourse. Melville's decision to reinsert the Nelson material, I propose, was designed to foreshadow the problem of critically assessing Vere and *his* position. Both Nelson and Vere invite subsequent criticism – Nelson by the "ornate publication of his person in battle" (Chap. 4, leaf 62) and Vere by hanging Billy Budd. Their parallel circumstances – questionable actions that incite later disputation – accentuate the inviolability of consciousness itself and the implacability of existential, if not heroic, choice. Melville's additions at *G* give focus to the narrator's declaration at *B* that "the *might-have-been* is but boggy ground to build on" (Chap. 4, leaf 65, Melville's italics). Historical reconstruction must avoid imposing the specious wisdom of hindsight on the drama of a living actor's private present.

The Nelson material and the warning against building on conjecture also prefigure the narrator's elaborations after Vere's drumhead court speech on the problematics of acting and thinking. The later fair-copy inscriptions need to be understood in relation to Melville's late revisions of early materials. By the time Melville reinserted the Nelson leaves, he had already inscribed (at F) Vere's speech as well as the narrator's brief but crucial discussion of the *Somers* mutiny.[16] While recognizing that the situations on the *Somers* and the *Bellipotent* "were different," the narrator argues that "the urgency felt, well-warranted or otherwise, was much the same" (Chap. 21, leaf 282). The focus is not on allegorized polarities but on crises of choice, the perplexities that inform, even as they entangle, the cognitive process. As he does elsewhere, the narrator quotes invented sources. Such fictive citations provide the appearance of authoritative corroboration. In an earlier version, the narrator cites "a writer whom nobody knows, and who being dead recks not of the oblivion" – certainly a wry self-portrait of Melville himself – not to vindicate Vere but to depict the arduous burden of choice. Revising in pencil, Melville deleted his mordant self-dramatization: "Says a writer whom few know, 'Forty years after a battle it is easy for a noncombatant to reason about how it ought to have been fought. It is another thing personally and under fire to have to direct the fighting while involved in the obscuring smoke of it. Much so with respect to other emergencies involving considerations both practical and moral, and when it is imperative promptly to act" (Chap. 21, leaves 282–83). Both Nelson and Vere, the first possessing "heroic personality" and the second "an exceptional character," provide posterity with challenging hermeneutical problems (Chap. 5, leaf 72 and Chap. 7, leaf 81). Persistently Melville's revisions situate the allegorical conflicts between Budd and Claggart, civilization and anarchy in relation to Vere's reaction. Belonging as they do to the later stages of inscription, the narrator's frequents acts of "indirection" – his digression and his cautionary citation, to name two – invite the reader to "cross the deadly space between" (Chap. 11, leaf 126), to pass from the easy-chair of latter-day prejudice into "the obscuring smoke" of imaginative self-engagement.

Melville's construction of Captain Vere's character stands as dialectical counterpoint to the tidy conclusion of the *B* inscription: "Here ends a story not unwarranted by what sometimes happens in this [ ] world of ours – Innocence and infamy, spiritual depravity and fair repute" (leaf 344). Ironically, Billy's "innocence" becomes "infamy"; Claggart's "spiritual depravity" becomes "fair repute." In this version, Billy's hanging simply happens. In the pencil draft stage *X*, Melville's development of Vere translated the ironic moral into a vexing question of incompatible imperatives. The problem of moral interpretation generates from the hierarchical arrangement of Vere's priorities: He is "an officer mindful of the welfare of his men, but never tolerating an infraction of discipline" (Chap. 6, leaf 74). In other words, the welfare of the "People" ends where discipline begins. The imperatives of moral or natural law – higher authorities, so to speak – are irrelevant to the non-transcendent dictates of the Mutiny Act. Vere's human heart subserves the war god. Had Melville been inclined to portray an incompetent or wicked sea-master, he could have reprised Captains Vangs (*Typee*), Guy (*Omoo*), Riga (*Redburn*), or Claret (*White-Jacket*). He might even have evoked the godly-demonical Ahab. A captain of Vere's peculiar dimensions is unprecedented in Melville's work. The "undemonstrative" Vere possesses a "resolute nature" which may – or may not – suggest "a virtue aristocratic in kind" (Chap. 6, leaves 77–78). Vere's thoughtful nature emerges in fits of abstracted pondering. A bookish man, at times reflecting "a serious mind of superior order," Vere is drawn to works "treating of actual men and events," not to speculative theology or romantic poetics. Vere has contempt for "cant and convention" and engages those writers "like

Montaigne, who . . . honestly and in the spirit of common sense philosophize upon those greatest of all mysteries, facts" (Chap. 6, leaves 82–83). In pencil, Melville crossed out "those . . . facts" and wrote "realities," a word that subsumes the mystery of facts but is less focused, more sweeping, lacking the paradoxical collision of opposites. The excised phrase might even imply the presence in Vere of a relativistic strain. A late pencil patch to leaf 83 accentuates the implications of "realities" and depicts Vere as an avowed conservative: "In this line of reading he found confirmation of his own more reserved thoughts – confirmation which he had vainly sought in social converse, so that as touching most fundamental topics, there had got to be established in him some positive convictions, which he forefelt would unalterably abide in him proof to all sophistries so long as his intelligent part remained unimpaired." At first it might seem odd that Melville deleted "proof to all sophistries." This fine phrase, however, might seem to express the narrator's unequivocal endorsement of Vere, which would amount to making Vere himself the locus of interpretive authority. The late pencil revisions removed not only the possibility that Vere could be construed as a relativist, but they opened the way to seeing Vere's decisive action as self-authorized and potentially sophistical. In the preceding chapter, Melville made a striking late pencil addition, also patched to the leaf, that similarly qualifies Vere's credibility. Regarding the captain's nickname, Starry Vere, Melville changed "How such a designation happened to fall to him was in this wise" to read "How such a designation happened to fall upon one who whatever his sterling qualities was without any brilliant ones" (Chap. 5, leaf 79). In revising Vere's portrait in light of his inscription of subsequent leaves, Melville worked toward a calculated ambiguity. Any single revision, especially Vere's lack of "brilliant" qualities, might seem to endorse an anti-Vere reading. But while the narrator qualifies Vere, he never denigrates him. In fact, Melville's revisions steadfastly avoided – and subverted – ideological homogeneity. The narrator's determinate statements coexist with the baffling implications of his indeterminate remarks. Characterizing Vere's portrait are the narrator's divided sympathies. Under Melville's revision, the narrator's unqualified endorsement elides into the mottled gray of irresolution. It is Vere's mind, one must recognize, that is preoccupied with "directness" and "settled convictions" (Chap. 7, leaves 83 and 87). The narrator's domain, on the contrary, partakes of "indirection," incompletion, and innuendo.

Interestingly, Billy shares Vere's quality of "directness," though the sailor's dissociation from acts or intimations of guile become hallmarks not of authority's insistence on "measured forms" but of the simple, easily duped tyro. In one instance, the narrator forges a dichotomy between the sailor as "frankness" and the landsman as "finesse. Life is not a game with the sailor, demanding the long head – no intricate game of chess where few moves are made in straightforwardness and ends are attained by indirection, an oblique, tedious, barren game hardly worth that poor candle burnt out in playing it" (Chap. 16, leaf 172). Inscribed at C, this passage belongs to that early stage where the narrator dramatizes the ironic triumph of "spiritual depravity" over "innocence." The narrator's bleak, angry assessment of civilization's burned-out waste offers stark testimony to the impracticability of innocence. To survive the involutions of fallen, landed life one must "exercise a distrust keen in proportion to the fairness of the appearance" (Chap. 16, leaf 174). The narrator seems to be referring here to individuals like himself "who know their kind in less shallow relations than business." Such "men of the world," paragons of "indirection," possess a "ruled, undemonstrative distrustfulness."

On the *Bellipotent*, such an attitude achieves expression in the anomalous Dansker. First appearing at *B* and developed further at *E* and *G*, the Dansker personifies the civilized marriage of prescience and detachment: To know is to have reason not to act. With his "small weasel eyes," the Dansker reflects at the level of dramatic action a diminutive version of the narrator himself. Characteristically, the Dansker recognizes Billy's beautiful, if perplexing, innocence. With his "eccentric unsentimental old sapience, primitive in its kind," the Dansker is atypical of the guileless sailor (Chap. 9, leaf 110). He is an insightful witness, a consciousness through which the narrator communicates deft surmises: His "quizzing sort of look . . . [was] sometimes replaced by an expression of speculative query as to what might eventually befall a nature like that, dropped into a world not without some mantraps and against whose subtleties simple courage lacking experience and address . . . is of little avail." Billy's plight evokes in the old man "a certain philosophic interest" (Chap. 9, leaves 110–11). The Dansker is a perceptive reader.[17] He lacks the "directness" associated with Vere and Billy. Or put another way, his direct statements flabbergast Billy. At stage *G*, the narrator presents an extended dialogue between Billy and the Dansker (Chap. 9, leaves 114–16). Informed without being enlightened, Billy hears that Claggart's "sweet voice" is indisputable evidence that he is "down upon" him. The Dansker will "commit himself to nothing further." Billy's inability to comprehend nuance makes him incapable of fathoming the Dansker's gnomic pronouncement. Of the men on the *Bellipotent*, the old sailor is the only one even remotely capable of warning Billy. But like Claggart and Vere, the Dansker is confined by the limitations of his nature. In *Billy Budd*, character becomes fate.[18] Individuals transcend neither their ontological endowments nor learned behavior. The Dansker could only have worked to avert Billy's tragedy had he somehow been other than who he is. In a late pencil addition, Melville made explicit the degree to which the Dansker's "sententious . . . Delphic deliverances" are not simply quaint, teasing suggestions but a philosophy of solipsistic self-preservation: "Long experience had very likely brought this old man to that bitter prudence which never interferes in aught and never gives advice" (Chap. 15, leaf 169). Just as Billy's nature is contained within Claggart's phrase, "[H]andsome is as handsome did it, too!" so too does the Dansker's cynical nature – his essence – dictate his inaction (Chap. 10, leaf 119). As Melville's revisions make clear, *Billy Budd* depicts the tragic intersection of incompatible characters, a collision in miniature of the sweeping force of historical necessity.

3

John Claggart poses the narrator's most daunting problem in character delineation. A late pencil patch preceding Claggart's introduction (inscribed at *B*) contains the narrator's admission of artistic incapacity: "His portrait I essay, but shall never hit it" (Chap. 8, leaf 88). In Chapter 11, the narrator's powerful speculation on Claggart's "inner personality," determinate statements provide points of departure into the unknown. In one of his more unequivocal utterances, the narrator validates the Dansker's assertion regarding Claggart's animosity toward Billy: "But, at heart and not for nothing, as the late chance encounter may indicate to the discerning, down on him, secretly down on him, he assuredly was" (Chap. 11, leaf 123). The early leaves of this chapter are very late additions. They attempt to make Claggart's malignity at least minimally comprehensible "to the discerning." A late pencil inscription testifies to the centrality of this endeavor: "The point of the present story turning on the hidden nature of the master-at-arms has necessitated this chapter" (leaf 135). The chapter's first movement concerns Claggart's "antipathy spontaneous" (leaf 125), toward Billy and the second movement presents the narrator's attempt to enter Claggart's "labyrinth" (leaf 127). Hayford and Sealts identify "labyrinth" as a "seed word" in Melville's "essay" on the phenomenology of Claggart's recondite nature.[19] In a discarded leaf, for example, the narrator remarks on the challenge of engaging Claggart's "inner personality": "One does not care to hazard getting lost in a dark labyrinth" (leaf 121A). At *G* he does hazard the attempt, first by asserting the "realism" of Claggart's ontological mystery, his "antipathy spontaneous and profound" (leaves 124 and 125), and then by traversing "the deadly space between" (leaf 126).

In passing from the quotidian to the exceptional, from what can be delineated to what can only be intuited, the narrator uses "indirection" and reconstructs a philosophical dialogue from many years before when he spoke with an "honest scholar." In considering the strange case of X, a prototype of Claggart, the scholar suggests that to "enter his labyrinth and get out again, without a clue derived from some source other than what is known as 'knowledge of the world' – that were hardly possible, at least for me" (leaf 127). The young man equates "knowledge of the world" with "knowledge of human nature," an equation which the scholar finds superficial: "I am not certain," he says, "whether to know the world and to know human nature be not two distinct branches of knowledge" (leaf 128). Ordinary activity "blunts that finer spiritual insight indispensable to the understanding of the essential in certain exceptional characters, whether evil ones or good" (leaf 129). In an early version, the narrator remarks, "At the time, I did not quite see the force of all this. I see it now." In pencil, Melville revised the passage to read: "At the time, my inexperience was such that I did not quite see the drift of all this. It may be that I see it now" (leaf 129). In replacing "force" with "drift," Melville accentuated the ambiguity of the narrator's present knowledge and highlighted his ongoing process of inquiry. The personal vignette from long ago dramatizes (indirectly) the provisional nature of his present tense hermeneutical foray. In constructing this epistemological paradigm, Melville unsettled the narrator's relation to his own knowledge. "It may be" that the narrator comprehends "the drift," but then again, it may not. To have retained the narrator's certitude would have been tantamount to making Claggart explicable. Instead, the narrator, standing as the reader's surrogate, enmeshes himself in the problem of deciphering the inscrutable and, in so doing, he depicts the mind in the act of thinking. He pursues the "exceptional" via the unreliable instrument of his own subjectivity; he is assisted only by textual resources that "might . . . define and denominate certain phenomenal men" (leaf 130). Such unpopular texts as Holy Writ and Plato's definition of natural depravity attempt to plumb the unfathomable mystery of innate iniquity.[20] The narrator can only suggest that the "mania" of an evil nature emerges not through a series of behavioral motives, but appears, phenomenally, as an act of nature. Thus, even Claggart might pine – as he seems to do in Chapter 12 – for the very innocence he abhors. Again, character is fate: He has "no power to annul the elemental evil in him . . . apprehending the good, but powerless to be it" (Chap. 12, leaf 142). The "elemental" force of Claggart's evil impels him to "act out to the end the part allotted it" (Chap. 12, leaf 142). In *Billy Budd* the determinations of fate constitute a fixed text that incites the provisional play of narrative "indirection."

Vere's fate is to become "nipped" in the interstices of Claggart's compulsion, a longing, it seems, to make Billy feel enmity, to experience "the reactionary bite of that serpent"

(Chap. 12, leaf 140). When Claggart appears on the quarter deck and lies about Billy's mutinous intentions, Vere confronts a herme neutical puzzle. He must construe the stark outlines of Claggart's questionable story in relation to a host of unsettling intimations. An "intuitional surmise" warns him against being "unduly disturbed by the general tenor of his subordinate's report" (Chap. 18, leaves 202–203). He perceives Claggart's tale, especially the warning to beware a "mantrap under the daisies" as "foggy" and self-condemnatory (Chap. 18, leaf 211). The narrator offers his most affirmative endorsement of Vere: "Though something exceptional in the moral quality of Captain Vere made him, in earnest encounter with a fellow man, a veritable touch stone of that man's essential nature, yet now as to Claggart and what was really going on in him his feeling partook less of intuitional conviction than of strong suspicion clogged by strange dubieties" (Chap. 18, leaf 214). Claggart taxes even Vere's prodigious powers of discernment. In attempting to read the meaning of Claggart's tale, Vere truly peruses a text that treats "of actual men and events" (leaves 82–83).

Vere's passion for "directness" prescripts his great unwitting error: staging a confrontation between Claggart and Budd. As audience and arbiter, Vere positions himself to "scrutinize the mutually confronting visages." Perhaps possessing a naive faith in the intrepid rectitude of his own perception, Vere perpetrates Billy's ambush. Claggart "deliberately advanced within short range of Billy and, mesmerically looking him in the eye, briefly recapitulated the accusation" (Chap. 19, leaf 221). Fittingly, this encounter contains the novel's imagistic culmination. Part of a late patched addition, "mesmerically" accentuates Claggart's serpentine attributes. Melville's revisions conflated Claggart's association with the "arch marplot of Eden" and his predatory nature. In describing the darkening of Claggart's dilating pupils, Melville changed "those lights of human intelligence" to "Adam's intelligence" before restoring the original figure. Linking Claggart with Adam would have confused the consistent imagery associating Billy with Adam. Only twelve leaves before, in a late pencil patch, Billy appears as one "who in the nude might have posed for a statue of young Adam before the Fall" (Chap. 18, leaf 208). Melville depicted not Claggart's fall from grace but his ontological devolution: "Those lights of human intelligence losing human expression, [were] gelidly protruding like the alien eyes of certain uncatalogued creatures of the deep." In another late pencil patch, Melville struggled with the figure: "The first mesmeristic glance was one of serpent fascination; the last threw up a stone wall." In revising the trope, Melville brilliantly replaced inert inscrutability with active malevolence: "the last was as the paralyzing lurch of the torpedo fish" (Chap. 19, leaf 222). After Billy strikes and kills Claggart and Vere exclaims, "Fated boy" (leaf 226), the narrator refuses to enter the Captain's psyche; he forgoes declarative statement in favor of an unanswered question: "Was [Vere] absorbed in taking in all the bearings of the event and what was best not only now at once to be done, but also in the sequel? (Chap. 19, leaf 227). This ambiguous formulation might stand as a prolegomenon to the many hundreds of pages assessing Vere's virtually instantaneous decision to hang Billy.

Melville himself was a troubled reader of Captain Vere. The most complicated, and significant, revisions of *Billy Budd* pertain to Melville's difficulties in presenting Vere's reactions to Billy, especially as they precipitate the surgeon's response. In question are six superseded leaves, which include the surgeon's initial identification with (and complementation of) Vere and the leaves that mistakenly stand as the "Preface" to all editions prior to Hayford and Sealts' Chicago edition.[21]

Throughout his revisions, Melville transformed determinate exposition into ambiguous dramatization. In canceled leaf 229a, the narrator unmistakably presents Billy as God's scourge of the wicked: "Yes, the young mute's blow, an athlete's, a blow elecrially energised by the spasm of his heart, unintentionally had had upon its object the all but instantanious operation of the divine judgement on Annannias [*sic*]." Assuming the office of narrative exposition, Vere calmly remarks, "Go now . . . before taking action I must have yet a few moments to mature the line of conduct I shall adopt. The case is no wonted one, nor could have happened at a worse time every way and for everybody more trying. A few moments for further thought and I shall act" (leaf 229b). In this version, the reasonable captain needs only some few moments to grapple with a "trying" situation. The surgeon concurs: "Too well the thoughtful officer knew what his superior meant." He considers how Vere's "utmost discretion" proves "more than futile" in "this human sphere subject as it is to unforseeable fatalities" (leaf 229c).

Melville realized his focus was all wrong. For one thing, Vere seems too calm and measured, too reasonable. By having the surgeon identify Vere as a victim of inadvertence and bad timing, Melville was blunting the tragic implications. The historical reconstruction of the "crisis for Christendom" (leaves 229d, e, f) rupture the unfolding drama. In a very late pencil addition, Vere loses his modulated calmness. Melville assigned Vere the narrator's trope. Excitedly, Vere blurts, "It is the divine judgment on Ananias!" (Chap. 19, leaf 231). Vere's next irruption – "Struck dead by an angel of God! Yet the angel must hang!" – reflects his summary conclusion (Chap. 19, leaf 232). By now, the "thoughtful" surgeon has become "prudent," a pejorative word in Melville's lexicon, bespeaking as it does the Dansker's cynical self-regard (leaf 231).

Perceiving Vere's outbursts as "mere incoherences," the surgeon becomes the first interpreter on the scene; "completely unapprised of the antecedents," he can only read surfaces (leaf 232). In Chapter 20, the surgeon's rumination about Vere's mental status – "Was he unhinged?" (leaf 235) – is reasonable given his ignorance. The surgeon, like "the lieutenants and captain of marines," believes that "such a matter should be referred to the admiral" (Chap. 20, leaves 235–36).

The narrator, however, considers the danger inherent in making judgments without adequate information – a danger that applies to Vere as well as his latter-day critics. In Chapter 21, the narrator wonders, "Who in the rainbow can draw the line where the violet tint ends and the orange tint begins?" (leaf 236). Who can, in other words, distinguish between the attenuated forms of sanity and the lesser degrees of madness? The answer is no one. Indeed, as Garner points out, in the spectrum, the violet and orange tints do not merge.[22] Between the violet and the orange lies another "deadly space" of yellow, green, blue, and indigo tints. The narrator associates the prudent surgeon with those "professional experts" who, for a fee, will "draw the exact line of demarcation," indeed will show exactly what in nature does not exist (leaf 236). While the surgeon concludes that Vere is "unhinged," the narrator refuses to specify what he thinks. In an early version, regarding the "supposition" that Vere is "the victim of aberration," the narrator declares, "I, for one, decline to determine." After revision, the narrator invites his readers to decide for themselves: "Whether Captain Vere, as the surgeon professionally and privately surmised, was really the sudden victim of any degree of aberration, every one must determine for himself by such light as this narrative may afford" (Chap. 21, leaf 237). To make the surgeon the locus of interpretive authority is to dismiss the broad range of possibility and ignore "deadly" spaces. It would explicitly give undue credit to the surgeon's lack of "antecedent" information, celebrate his penchant for making quick judgments, and disregard, as Chapter 26 reveals, his inane pedantry. The essence of Melville's revision is to place the burden of judgment on the reader, a position that seems the natural issue of Melville's earlier complication of allegory. Thus reading *Billy Budd* becomes less a matter of blaming or exonerating Vere and more a process of apprehending the accumulation of terrible complexities, especially Vere's conviction that moral questions are irrelevant to the demands of *realpolitik*: "The essential right and wrong involved in the matter, the clearer that might be, so much the worse for the responsibility of the loyal sea commander, inasmuch as he was not authorized to determine the matter on that primitive basis" (Chap. 21, leaves 239–40). *Billy Budd* dramatizes a complex that animates Melville's philosophical thought in *Typee*, *Mardi*, *Moby-Dick*, *Pierre*, *The Confidence-Man*, and *Clarel* – the dissociation between heavenly truth and earthly convention, chronometricals and horologicals, and noumenal and phenomenal realms.[23] With Vere, the narrator seems to be demonstrating how the fated compulsions of character dictate self-defeat: Vere is guilty of responding to the world in the hardened terms of his mind's habitual use. He cannot stand outside the narrow perimeter, or rut, of his consciousness. His characteristic "directness" finds a terrifying complement in his flawed comprehension of the Mutiny Act.[24] Without question, Vere makes egregious errors in his application of this law, especially as he believes it prescribes the polarized choice, condemn or let go. A nagging, and so far unanswered, question in *Billy Budd* criticism involves whether Melville *knew* that Vere was wrong. Simply put, Vere believes he must hang the innocent or risk anarchy. What the reader seems invited to "determine" is the worth of a civilization that demands this sacrifice.

At the level of dramatic action, Melville made revisions that accentuated the oppressive entanglement of historical forces. Disputations over the propriety of the drumhead court are moot; Vere has already made up his mind: "The angel must hang." One of Vere's "measured forms," the trial allows Vere to lecture on the incompatibility between public duty and private conviction. He lays out the issues with his customary directness. The primitive, or primal, elements of human nature are inimical to Force. As an officer Vere inhabits a monistic world bereft of nuance. A martial court can only focus on the blow's consequence and has nothing to do with "a matter for psychologic theologians" (Chap. 21, leaf 259). On the contrary, the narrator's province includes the speculative domain of dialectic. Significantly, while betraying sympathy for Vere's plight, the narrator takes no stand on whether Vere should hang Billy. Vere's decision to execute Billy co-exists with the narrator's depiction of Vere's suffering "the agony of the strong" (Chap. 22, leaf 289). In quoting the writer "whom few know," the narrator highlights the tenuousness of existential choice, the hazard involved in having to "direct the fighting while involved in the obscuring smoke of it" (Chap. 21, leaf 282). "Indirection" constitutes the narrator's primary means of recreating the "obscuring smoke" of a distant historical moment. The narrator's elusiveness also excites the many unanswered questions that inform *Billy Budd* criticism.

Vere's public duty envelopes primitive suffering, a circumstance that leaves the narrator outside, rather than privy to, the closeted interview between Vere and Billy. The narrator admits that there is no language – "no telling the sacrament" – capable of expressing what happens when "two of great Nature's nobler order embrace" (Chap. 22, leaf 288). Such a conjunction must remain inviolate, indeed "all but incredible to average minds however much cultivated" (Chap. 22, leaf 286). Nevertheless, the narrator ventures "some conjectures": "Captain Vere in end may have developed the passion sometimes latent under an exterior stoical or indifferent. He was old enough to have been Billy's father. The austere devotee of military duty, letting himself melt back into what remains primeval in our formalized humanity, may in end have caught Billy to his heart, even as Abraham may have caught young Isaac on the brink of resolutely offering him up in obedience to the exacting behest" (Chap. 22, leaves 287–88). The narrator's subjunctive verbs are speculative corollaries to the tendency of Melville's revisions. Here the narrator imagines a possible action and its typological counterpart, both of which remain imaginative postulants and therefore dramatic absences, perhaps no more than the narrator's fond fancy. He calls attention to the diminutive authority of his *"might-have-been"* and accentuates the implacable barrier that shields an actor's most private life. One may venture into this "space" only by way of a fiction, a speculation in the subjunctive mode. The narrator participates in the very activity that all readers must engage.

4

Thirty-nine years before he died, in first exploring the possibilities of third person narrative in *Pierre* (1852), Melville anticipated the "indirection" of *Billy Budd*. Not only does *Pierre*'s narrator often use present tense to mediate between determinate and indeterminate positions, but he also criticizes "false" novels that make "inverted attempts at systematizing eternally unsystemizable elements; their audacious, intermeddling impotency, in trying to unravel, and spread out, and classify, the more thin than gossamer threads which make up the complex web of life." Conversely, the narrator celebrates a fictional mode that dramatizes the sprawling irresolution of life and views such works as "the profounder emanations of the human mind." Such "attempts" eschew conventions of closure: They "never unravel their own intricacies, and have no proper endings; but in imperfect, unanticipated, and disappointing sequels (as mutilated stumps), hurry to abrupt intermergings in the eternal tides of time and fate."[25] In depicting contingent confusion, the "profounder" books end with jolts and ruptures.

The narrator of *Billy Budd*, though less (overtly) contemptuous of symphonic closure, nevertheless makes a similar distinction between "[t]he symmetry of form attainable in pure fiction" and a "narration essentially having less to do with fable than with fact. Truth uncompromisingly told will always have its ragged edges; hence the conclusion of such a narrative is apt to be less finished than an architectural finial" (Chap. 28, leaf 335). *Billy Budd*'s conclusion, the narrator suggests, will be more true because it retains the "ragged edges" of the life-as-lived as well as the impenetrable veil of a distant historical time. At one point, however, Melville intended to trim one "ragged" edge. The "News from the Mediterranean" presents a distorted though "authorized" version of events. Billy appears as a depraved criminal and Claggart his patriotic victim. The official account makes no mention of Vere's role or his recent death. Obviously, Vere did not figure in the narrative when "News" was first inscribed. Later, in pencil, at the top of leaf 340, Melville wrote, "Speak of the fight + death of Captain Vere." Apparently, Melville intended to work Vere into the "News." The fact that Vere was never included may seem a simple case of Melville not living to make the addition. Significantly, however, he *canceled the note*, deciding against mentioning Vere at all. Melville's choice has telling implications: Vere's exclusion from the official record precipitates the

need for an "inside narrative"; moreover, Vere's absence accentuates the ironic futility of his attempts to ensure the stability of "lasting institutions." The canceled note effaces Vere's
place in the official record and translates him into an historical
nullity. However meritorious or meretricious, Vere's intentions and actions have no effect. Thus the "ragged" contours
of the "inside narrative" function as a dialectical counterpoint
to the authorized account and the sentimentalized fable, "Billy
in the Darbies." Fittingly, the poem that propelled Melville's
years of continuing complication stands as a haunting coda
to the still uncompleted tale of "innocence" enmeshed by
"infamy."[26]

NOTES

1 *Billy Budd, Sailor (An Inside Narrative)*, eds. Harrison Hayford and
   Merton M. Sealts, Jr. (University of Chicago Press, 1962), Chap. 21,
   leaves 246–47. This volume contains the reading text and the genetic
   text of *Billy Budd*. The nature of this study requires that references
   be cited by chapter and leaf.
2 Robert Milder, "Introduction," in *Critical Essays on Melville's Billy
   Budd, Sailor*, ed. Robert Milder (Boston: G. K. Hall, 1989), p. 1.
3 Milder summarizes the dichotomous nature of the criticism: "Like
   'Platonist or Aristotelian,' 'conservative or radical,' the tale separates its readers into timeless parties of the mind, though not without
   allowing them their distinct temporal coloring of method and ide-
   ology." Ibid. For evenhanded, incisive overviews of *Billy Budd*'s
   complex and acerbic critical history, see Ibid. pp. 3–18 and Sealts,
   "Innocence and Infamy: *Billy Budd, Sailor*," in *A Companion to
   Melville Studies*, ed. John Bryant (New York: Greenwood Press,
   1986), pp. 407–30. *Billy Budd* criticism properly begins with E. L.
   Grant Watson, "Melville's Testament of Acceptance," *New England
   Quarterly* 6 (June 1933): 319–27.
4 For the most compelling pro-Vere position, see Milton R. Stern,
   The Fine Hammered Steel of Herman Melville (Urbana: University
   of Illinois Press, 1957), pp. 206–39, and Stern's "Introduction" to
   Billy Budd, Sailor (Indianapolis: Bobbs-Merrill, 1975), pp. xi–xliv.

5 Anti-Vere positions often appear as "ironist" readings. Notable discussions include Joseph Schiffman, "Melville's Final Stage, Irony: A Reexamination of *Billy Budd* Criticism," *American Literature* 22 (May 1950): 128–36; Karl E. Zink, "Herman Melville and the Forms – Irony and Social Criticism in 'Billy Budd.'" *Accent* 12 (Summer 1952): 131–39; Phil Withim, "*Billy Budd*: Testament of Resistance," *Modern Language Quarterly* 20 (June 1959): 115–27; Kingsley Widmer, "*Billy Budd* and Conservative Nihilism," in his *The Ways of Nihilism: A Study of Herman Melville's Short Novels* (Los Angeles: Ward-Ritchie Press, 1970), pp. 16–58; Stanton A. Garner, "Fraud as Fact in Herman Melville's *Billy Budd*," *San Jose Studies* 4 (May 1978): 82–105.

6 For a consideration of Melville's identification with the narrator, see Sealts "Innocence and Infamy," 412; for discussions of Melville's detachment from the narrator, see James Duban, "The Cross of Consciousness: *Billy Budd*," in *Melville's Major Fiction: Politics, Theology, and Imagination* (Dekalb: Northern Illinois University Press, 1983), pp. 221–48; Thomas J. Scorza, *In the Time before Steamships: Billy Budd, The Limits of Politics, and Modernity* (Dekalb: Northern Illinois University Press, 1979), pp. 4–7; Garner, "Fraud as Fact," 86–94.

7 See Widmer, *The Ways of Nihilism*, pp. 16–24 for the dangers of allegory and fixed interpretive polarities.

8 Parker, *Reading Billy Budd* (Evanston: Northwestern University Press, 1990), p. 91.

9 Hayford and Sealts, *Billy Budd*, p. 35, their italics. The genesis of *Billy Budd* is not a reflection of thematic succession. As my discussion makes clear, I disagree with Milder's claim that *Billy Budd* "remains a thematically sequential work whose shifts of interest replicate its compositional history and reflect Melville's inward journey over the last five years of his life" ("Melville's Late Poetry and *Billy Budd*: From Nostalgia to Transcendence," in Milder, *Critical Essays*, p. 213).

10 For discussions of Melville's fictionalization of history, see Sealts, "Innocence and Infamy," p. 419; James McIntosh, "*Billy Budd, Sailor*: Melville's Last Romance," in Milder, *Critical Essays*, p. 226; Garner, "Fraud as Fact," p. 87.

11 For discussions of indeterminacy in *Billy Budd*, see Paul Brodtkorb, Jr., "The Definitive *Billy Budd*: 'But Aren't It All Sham?'" *PMLA*

82 (December 1967): 600–12; Barbara Johnson, "Melville's Fist: The Execution of *Billy Budd*," *Studies in Romanticism* 18 (Winter 1979): 567–99.

12 For an excellent treatment of the relationship between genealogy and identity in Melville's works, see Peter J. Bellis, *No Mysteries Out of Ourselves: Identity and Textual Form in the Novels of Herman Melville* (Philadelphia: University of Pennsylvania Press, 1990).

13 *Moby-Dick or The Whale*, eds. Harrison Hayford, Hershel Parker, and G. Thomas Tanselle (Chicago and Evanston: Northwestern University Press and The Newberry Library, 1988), p. 205.

14 For discussions of Nelson, see Stern, *The Fine Hammered Steel*, pp. 208–10; Ralph W. Willet, "Nelson and Vere: Hero and Victim in *Billy Budd, Sailor*," *PMLA* 82 (October 1967): 370–6; Merlin Bowen, "[Captain Vere and the Weakness of Expediency]," in Milder, *Critical Essays*, pp. 69–70; and Parker, *Reading Billy Budd*, pp. 110–13.

15 See Hayford and Sealts, *Billy Budd*, pp. 245–46.

16 For discussions of the *Somers* mutiny, see Michael Paul Rogin, "The *Somers* Mutiny and *Billy Budd*: Melville in the Penal Colony," in *Herman Melville*, ed. Harold Bloom (New York: Chelsea House, 1986), pp. 197–221; and Duban, *Melville's Major Fiction*, pp. 238–43.

17 For discussions of the Dansker as reader, see Stern, *The Fine Hammered Steel*, 219–20; Sharon Baris, "Melville's Dansker: The Absent Daniel in *Billy Budd*," in *The Uses of Adversity: Failure and Accommodation in Reader Response*," ed. Ellen Spolsky (Lewisburg, PA: Bucknell University Press, 1990), pp. 153–73.

18 For an early expression of Melville's articulation of character as fate, see *White-Jacket or The World in a Man-of-War*, eds. Harrison Hayford, Hershel Parker, and G. Thomas Tanselle (Evanston and Chicago: Northwestern University Press and The Newberry Library, 1970), pp. 320–21.

19 Hayford and Sealts, *Billy Budd*, p. 253.

20 For a discussion of the narrator's dialogue with the scholar, see Scorza, *In the Time before Steamships*, pp. 77–80.

21 For discussions of the so-called "Preface," see Hayford and Sealts, *Billy Budd*, 18–19; and Parker, *Reading Billy Budd*, pp. 86–89. Stern incorporates the "preface" into his edition; he places superseded leaves 229d, 229e, and 229f after leaf 238. For his cogent explanation of this restoration, see Stern, *Billy Budd*, pp. 152–55.

22 See Garner, "Fraud as Fact," 94.

23 For a discussion of the philosophical implications of this complex, see John Wenke, "'Ontological Heroics': Melville's Philosophical Art," in Bryant, *A Companion to Melville Studies*, pp. 567–601; John Wenke, *Melville's Muse: Literary Creation and the Forms of Philosophical Fiction* (Kent, Ohio: Kent State University Press, 1995).

24 On the legal aspects of Vere's predicament, see Hayford and Sealts, *Billy Budd*, pp. 180–83, notes 272–81; C. B. Ives, "*Billy Budd* and the Articles of War," *American Literature* 34 (1962): 31–39; Sealts, "Innocence and Infamy," 417–19.

25 *Pierre or The Ambiguities*, eds. Harrison Hayford, Hershel Parker, and G. Thomas Tanselle (Evanston and Chicago: Northwestern University Press and The Newberry Library, 1971), p. 141.

26 For a related study of the genetic text, see John Wenke, "Complicating Vere: Melville's Practice of Revision in *Billy Budd*," *Leviathan* 1 (March 1999), 83–88.

Select bibliography

This listing is quite selective because *Billy Budd* criticism has been so plentiful that several collections have been issued since the late 1960s with the purpose of reflecting trends in interest and interpretation by reprinting extracts of significant contributions or entire essays or chapters (only infrequently offering new studies). The volumes (in chronological order) are by Stafford, Springer, Vincent, and Milder. Overviews of the critical history are offered in the Hayford and Sealts "Editors' Introduction," Sealts's "Innocence and Infamy," Milder's "Introduction," and the early chapters of Parker's interpretive discussion. Use of these and perhaps other bibliographies and reviews, while making this listing more manageable than it would be were it more comprehensive, will provide the reader with shortcuts to what are generally the best and/or most representative criticism and interpretation.

For thorough listings, see Higgins's annotated bibliography, the annual *PMLA Bibliography*, and the more selective Melville chapter in *American Literary Scholarship: An Annual*, which provides discussion of a given reviewer's judgments.

Unless otherwise noted, references to Melville's work in this volume are to Harrison Hayford and Merton M. Sealts, Jr., eds. *Billy Budd, Sailor (An Inside Narrative)*. University of Chicago Press, 1962. Others are to "The Writings of Herman Melville" in progress: Evanston and Chicago, Ill.: Northwestern University Press and The Newberry Library (N/N).

Anderson, Charles Roberts. "The Genesis of *Billy Budd*." *American Literature* 12 (1940): 329–46.
Berthoff, Warner. *The Example of Melville*. Princeton University Press, 1962.

Bryant, John. *Melville Dissertations, 1924–1980: An Annotated Bibliography and Subject Index*. Westport and London: Greenwood Press, 1980.

Cohen, Hennig, and Donald Yannella. *Herman Melville's Malcolm Letter: "Man's Final Lore."* New York: Fordham University Press and The New York Public Library, 1992.

Fogle, Richard Harter. *"Billy Budd* – Acceptance or Irony." *Tulane Studies in English* 8 (1958): 107–13.

    "Billy Budd: The Order of the Fall." *Nineteenth-Century Fiction* 15 (1960): 189–205. Rpt. Milder.

Garner, Stanton. "Fraud as Fact in Herman Melville's *Billy Budd*." *San Jose Studies* 4 (1978): 82–105.

Hayford, Harrison, ed. *The Somers Mutiny Affair*. Englewood Cliffs, N.J.: Prentice-Hall, 1959.

Hays, Peter L., and Richard Dilworth Rust. "'Something Healing': Fathers and Sons in *Billy Budd*." *Nineteenth-Century Fiction* 34 (1979): 326–36.

Higgins, Brian. *Herman Melville: A Reference Guide, 1931–1960*. Boston, Mass.: G.K. Hall, 1987.

Milder, Robert, ed. *Critical Essays on Melville's "Billy Budd, Sailor."* Boston, Mass.: G.K. Hall, 1989.

Miller, Edwin Haviland. *Melville*. New York: Braziller, 1975.

Murray, Charles. "A Concordance to Melville's *Billy Budd*." PhD Diss., Miami University, 1979.

Parker, Hershel. *Reading Billy Budd*. Evanston, Ill.: Northwestern University Press, 1990.

Reich, Charles A. "The Tragedy of Justice in *Billy Budd*." *Yale Review* 56 (1967) 368–89. Rpt. Milder.

Rosenberry, Edward H. "The Problem of *Billy Budd*." *PMLA* 80 (1965): 489–98.

Scorza, Thomas J. *In the Time before Steamships: Billy Budd, the Limits of Politics, and Modernity*. DeKalb: Northern Illinois University, 1979.

Sealts, Merton M., Jr. "Innocence and Infamy: *Billy Budd, Sailor*." In John Bryant, ed. *A Companion to Melville Studies*. New York: Greenwood Press, 1986: 407–30.

    Pursuing Melville: Chapters and Essays. Madison: University of Wisconsin Press, 1982.

Springer, Haskell, comp. *The Merrill Studies in Billy Budd*. Columbus, Ohio: Merrill, 1970.

Stafford, William T., ed. *Melville's Billy Budd and the Critics*. Belmont, Calif.: Wadsworth, 1968.

Stern, Milton R., ed. and introd. *Billy Budd, Sailor (An Inside Narrative)*. Indianapolis: Bobbs-Merrill, 1975.

Thompson, Lawrance. *Melville's Quarrel with God*. Princeton University Press, 1952.

Vincent, Howard P., ed. *Twentieth Century Interpretations of Billy Budd: A Collection of Critical Essays*. Englewood Cliffs, N.J.: Prentice-Hall, 1971.

Widmer, Kingsley. "The Perplexed Myths of Melville: *Billy Budd*." *Novel* 2 (1968): 25–35.

Willett, Ralph W. "Nelson and Vere: Hero and Victim in *Billy Budd, Sailor*." *PMLA* 82 (1967): 370–76.

Withim, Phil. "*Billy Budd*: Testament of Resistance." *Modern Language Quarterly* 20 (1959): 115–27.

Index